Public-Private Partnerships in the USA

T0341024

Broadly, a public-private partnership (or PPP) is any collaboration between the public and private sector, but research in the UK has tended to focus on those that have been used for major infrastructure projects, such as roads, schools and hospitals. This book compares and contrasts PPP research in the UK with that of cases in the USA, including interviews with some of the key stakeholders (decision makers in the public sector, contractors and users) of PPPs in North America, and observations of PPPs in action (such as schools and roads).

No prior major studies have compared the UK and USA when it comes to the development and operation of PPPs, and this book fills a gap in the literature, addressing a number of key questions, including: Is the private sector viewed with less suspicion in the USA when it comes to projects that would normally fall under the aegis of the public sector? How do politics affect PPPs? How do key players in the PPP process define project success, determine the merits and drawbacks of the initiative, and deal with controversial elements of the scheme such as value for money and risk transfer? The result is a volume that offers practical advice for the future development of PPPs in the UK.

Anthony Wall is a senior lecturer in the Ulster Business School, University of Ulster, UK. He joined the university as a research assistant in 1999 following a variety of jobs in both the public and private sectors. He was appointed a lecturer in 2000 and a senior lecturer in 2007. He was awarded the Fulbright Northern Ireland Public Sector Fellowship in 2010.

Routledge Critical Studies in Public Management

Edited by Stephen Osborne

Public-Private Partnerships in the USA

Lessons to be Learned for the United Kingdom

Anthony Wall

Routledge
Taylor & Francis Group

NEW YORK AND LONDON

First published in paperback 2024

First published 2013
by Routledge
605 Third Avenue, New York, NY 10158

and by Routledge
4 Park Square, Milton Park, Abingdon, Oxon OX14 4RN

Routledge is an imprint of the Taylor & Francis Group, an informa business

Library of Congress Cataloging-in-Publication Data

Wall, Tony.
   Public-private partnerships in the USA : lessons to be learned for the
United Kingdom / by Tony Wall.
      p. cm. — (Routledge critical studies in public management ; 8)
      Includes bibliographical references and index.
   1. Public-private sector cooperation—United States.   2. Public-private
sector cooperation—Great Britain.   I. Title.
   HD3872.U6.W35   2012
   338.8—dc23
   2012035926

ISBN: 978-0-415-81879-7 (hbk)
ISBN: 978-1-03-293039-8 (pbk)
ISBN: 978-0-203-38772-6 (ebk)

DOI: 10.4324/9780203387726

Typeset in Sabon
by Apex CoVantage, LLC

Contents

Abbreviations

AN	Application Note
ASSIST	American Stop Smoking Intervention Study
ATIS	Advanced Traveller Information Systems
ATP	Advanced Technology Program
BID	Business Improvement District
BLC	Business Leadership Coalition
BOO	Build, Own, Operate
BOT	Build, Operate, Transfer
BSF	Building Schools for the Future
BTO	Build, Transfer, Operate
BWI	Baltimore Washington International Thurgood Marshall (Airport)
CEO	Chief Executive Officer
CFP	Casey Family Programs
CGIAR	Consultative Group on International Agricultural Research
CMOHI	Central Massachusetts Oral Health Initiative
CTC	City Technology College
DB	Design and Build
DBFO	Design, Build, Finance and Operate
DBO	Design, Build, Operate
DBOM	Design, Build, Operate and Maintain
DC	District of Columbia
DoD	Department of Defense
EAZ	Education Action Zone
EMO	Education Management Organisation
EPA	Environmental Protection Agency
FHwA	Federal Highway Administration
GAO	General Accounting Office
GTP	GlobalTransPark
HMO	Health Maintenance Organisation
HMT	Her Majesty's Treasury
HOT	High Occupancy Toll
HOV	High Occupancy Vehicle

I-	Interstate-
IFRIC	International Financial Reporting Interpretations Committee
IP	Intellectual Property
IPPR	Institute of Public Policy Research
IT	Information Technology
KPIs	Key Performance Indicators
LACDB	Los Angeles Community Development Bank
LEA	Local Education Authority
LIFT	Local Improvement Finance Trust
MCO	Managed Care Organisation
MoD	Ministry of Defence
NAO	National Audit Office
NCPPPs	National Council for Public-Private Partnerships
NCSL	National Conference of State Legislatures
NEPSI	National Electronics Product Stewardship Initiative
NGO	Non-Government Organisation
NHS	National Health Service
NIAO	Northern Ireland Audit Office
NPD	Non-Profit Distribution
OECD	Organisation for Economic Co-operation and Development
PBF	Prudential Borrowing Framework
PFI	Private Finance Initiative
PILOT	Payment in Lieu of Taxes
PPP	Public Private Partnership
PSC	Public Sector Comparator
PVR	Present-Value-of-Revenue
PWF	Public Works Financing
R&D	Research and Development
RECLAIM	Los Angeles Regional Clean Air Incentives Market
SCDOT	South Carolina Department of Transportation
SESS	Starting Early Starting Smart
SFT	Scottish Futures Trust
SPV	Special Purpose Vehicle
SRP	Strategic Research Partnership
SR 91	California Orange County State Route 91
TIF	Tax Increment Financing
TIFIA	Transportation Infrastructure Finance and Innovation Act
TIRZ	Tax Increment Reinvestment Zone
UK	United Kingdom
USA	United States of America
USDOT	USA's Department of Transportation
VDOT	Virginia Department of Transportation
VFM	Value for Money
WMATA	Washington Metropolitan Area Transit Authority
WTO	World Trade Organisation

Acknowledgments

The author wishes to express his gratitude to the Fulbright Commission for kindly sponsoring his research study in the USA and for its ongoing support. He would also like to thank the Trachtenberg School of Public Policy and Public Administration, George Washington University, for hosting his stay in the USA. In particular he would like to thank Professor James Kee from this institution, who provided valuable guidance throughout the visit. Thanks as well to those individuals whose comments and views are reported in Chapters Seven, Eight and Nine of this book, who kindly agreed to be interviewed. Finally he would like to thank the University of Ulster for allowing him the time off work to study in the USA.

1   Introduction

The aim of this book is to compare the usage and current state of public-private partnerships (PPPs) in the United States of America (USA) with that of the United Kingdom (UK). The author was fortunate enough to travel to the USA and observe some of the many PPPs in progress or in operation and also interview some of the key stakeholders in the PPP process, including government officials, private contractors, users of PPPs and academics. The latter group is seen as important as the context of this book is fundamentally academic, with the literature reviewed being primarily journal articles and texts; however, other sources such as newspaper articles, government reports and non-academic publications have also been used. The aim of the study was to establish if the UK, the government of which appears to have taken a far more cautious approach to using PPPs as a method of infrastructure development, could learn anything from the much wider usage of PPPs in the USA. Moreover, why have the academic communities taken such a different stance towards PPPs? On the face of it the scheme seems more acceptable in the USA, whereas in the UK it has never received much support.

To my knowledge no major studies have ever compared the UK and USA when it comes to the development and operation of PPPs. Fitz and Beers (2002) looked at what they saw as the privatisation of education in both countries, but did not look beyond this sector. Two US academics, Kee and Forrer (2008), investigated the UK's Private Finance Initiative (PFI), but did not set out to compare and contrast the model with PPPs in the USA. PPPs continue to be controversial in the UK despite a number of changes introduced in order to both speed up the contractual negotiation stages and improve the profit-sharing arrangements between the various partners. However, they are less controversial in other countries and thus comparisons are useful. International reviews of PPP projects in themselves are fairly sparse, with ones by Hodge and Greve (2007) and Grimsey and Lewis (2005) only really touching on very broad issues. Moreover, Dumort (2000) compared the use of social media in secondary and higher education in the USA and European Union, suggesting that PPPs would be an effective way of maximising its potential. This study is therefore seen as significant as it will compare the general use of PPPs in a region where the use of the private sector in public-sector infrastructure projects and service provision has always been viewed with a certain amount of suspicion with one where the private sector has traditionally had a much greater involvement with projects of this nature.

Accordingly, the objectives of the study are to try to answer the following questions:

- How has the PPP process evolved in the USA? Are there major differences when it comes to the use of PPPs between different states?
- Is the private sector viewed with less suspicion in the USA when it comes to projects that would normally fall under the aegis of the public sector? Is this due to different political systems, with the neo-liberal, free market thinking still more in favour in the USA?
- Are public-sector employees in the USA better when it comes to negotiation with private-sector partners? There is a suspicion that UK public-sector employees are often at a disadvantage when dealing with contractors and their consultants, due to reservoirs of expertise not being built up in more commercial areas.
- How do key players in the PPP process in the USA define project success; determine the merits and drawbacks of the initiative; and deal with controversial elements of the scheme in the UK such as value for money and risk transfer?
- Are there any areas of good practice or lessons that can be learnt for the future development of PPPs in the UK?

Before embarking on any text on PPPs it is perhaps important to define exactly what they are, although this is not a simple task. There are many different definitions of what constitutes a PPP (see, for example, Garvin, 2010, p. 404), with the United Nations General Assembly (2005, p. 4) defining them as 'voluntary and collaborative relationships between various parties, both State and non-State, in which all participants agree to work together to achieve a common purpose or undertake a specific task and to share risk and responsibilities, resources and benefits'. Going by its broadest definition, a PPP can be any collaboration between the public and private sectors—for example, a school contracting out its catering to a private enterprise; however, there is some debate whether contracting out constitutes a partnership. Under certain conditions, where there is no shared risk taking or development of ideas, the arrangement seems to be more of a traditional contract. Peters (1998) stated that there were five points that characterised a PPP:

1. The partnership must involve two or more actors, at least one of which is a public entity;
2. Each of the participating actors must be able to bargain on its own behalf;
3. The partnership involves a long-term, enduring relationship,

Table 1.1 The DBFO Model and its Variants (Adapted from Grimsey and Lewis, 2004)

Term	Description
Build, own, operate (BOO)	The developer is responsible for design, funding, construction, operation and maintenance of the facility during the concession period, with no provision for transfer of ownership to the government. At the end of the concession period, the original agreement may be renegotiated, a new agreement may be negotiated, or the facility may be purchased by the government.
Build, own, operate, transfer	An arrangement where a facility is designed, financed, operated and maintained by a concession company. Ownership rests with the concessionaire until the end of the concession period, at which point ownership and operating rights are transferred to the government (normally without charge).
Build, operate, transfer (BOT)	An agreement where a facility is designed, financed, operated and maintained by the concessionaire for the period of the concession. Legal ownership of the facility may or may not rest with the concession company.
Design, build, finance, operate (DBFO)	The main form of contract in the PFI whereby the service provider is responsible for the design, construction, financing and operation of an asset. Operation refers to the provision of some or all of the services related to the asset's use.
Design, build, operate (DBO)	A form of PPP, in which the public sector provides finance for a capital investment project, but the providers of the projects retain the design and construction, and deliver some or all of the operational elements.

4. Each actor must be able to bring either material or symbolic goods to the relationship; and
5. All actors must have a shared responsibility for the outcomes of the partnership.

In the author's opinion, there are two other factors that distinguish a PPP from other arrangements: there has got to be some sort of return for the private sector, be it financial or non-financial in the form of marketing or brand awareness; and the private sector must be taking on a role that hitherto was carried out by the public sector. If these two factors are not part of the agreement then it is either charity or a form of corporate social responsibility on behalf of the private partner or a normal commercial arrangement (see the example of the use of Web 2.0 tools ahead). Notwithstanding, for the purposes of the UK part of this report, a PPP refers to the design, build, finance and operate (DBFO) model or its variants (see Table 1.1), although it is not the only use of PPP in this country (see McQuaid and Scherrer, 2010).

There are also several different types of PPP, which are used to achieve varying outcomes. Brinkerhoff and Brinkerhoff (2011, pp. 6–7) categorise these types in the following way:

- Policy PPPs, which seek to design, advocate for, coordinate or monitor public policies of various types;
- Service delivery PPPs, which engage non-state actors in delivering public services;
- Infrastructure PPPs, which bring together governments and the private sector to finance, build and operate infrastructure such as highways and sewage and waste treatment facilities;
- Capacity building PPPs, which can address service delivery needs or more explicitly focus on helping to develop the skills, systems and capabilities that allow groups and organisations that have been targeted for assistance to help themselves; and
- Economic development PPPs, which are cross-sectoral collaborations that promote economic growth and poverty reduction.

This book will focus mainly on PPPs that come under the umbrella of service delivery, infrastructure and economic development, although examples of the other two will be provided in Chapters Three to Six. Moreover, one of the interviewees in Chapter Seven is involved in capacity building.

It is also worth mentioning at this stage that the term 'private' in the USA definition of PPP does not always, but often does, denote a profit-making organisation (see, for example, Lovrich, 1999; Moulton and Anheier, 2001). However, for the purposes of this study the term private will indicate a private-sector, profit-making organisation. Therefore, PPPs in which the private partner is a religious entity (see, for example, Minow, 2003; Yancey et al., 2004) or a non-profit agency providing social services (see, for example, Hill, 2002; Morland et al., 2005; Oakley, 2006) will not be covered in the literature review. Likewise sometimes the word 'private' is used to refer to a private individual giving up his or her spare time to help a public-sector organisation become more effective in some area, but such a meaning will not be relevant to this study. Another area of ambiguity could arise from different uses of the word 'privatisation'; in the USA privatisation is defined as any shift in the locus of the production of services from public to private, whereas in the UK it means the explicit transfer of public assets to private ownership (Grimsey and Lewis, 2005). There are also instances where some research has referred to PPPs, when in fact the public sector is merely using a private-sector supplier as no public-sector organisation is capable of providing a similar service. For example, Hui and Hayllar (2010) give several examples of US public organisations making use of Web 2.0 tools (e.g., YouTube, Facebook, Google maps, Twitter) to better engage with its citizens. Whilst the authors suggest benefits such as the provision of 'fresh opportunities and new ways for governments, the private sector and citizens to collaborate together' (p. s128), it is debatable whether the use of the technology provided by global organisations by governments really constitute PPPs. Likewise, Schuster and Lundstrom (2002) analysed the role of the US government in international trade, stating that it had an interest in promoting the exports of private companies as this usually adds to the wealth of a nation. However, despite the authors labelling such arrangements as PPPs, it could be argued that such activity comes under the umbrella of normal government duties. Finally, PPPs are sometimes referred to as P3s in the USA, although the term will not be used in this study.

The book is laid out as follows. Chapter Two gives a very broad overview of PPPs in the UK; it is not intended to be a thorough review of all PPP activity and could never hope to capture the huge amount of research. However, it will hopefully provide a starting point for the far more in-depth literature review of PPPs in the USA in the following four chapters. Moreover, UK literature will be covered in Chapters Three to Six, whenever it complements or appears to contradict that of the USA. It is worth stating that although the review of the US literature is comprehensive, it by no means covers everything written on the subject. The aim is to provide a good overview of what sectors are being studied and the differing viewpoints of academics in the USA regarding PPPs. Chapter Three gives a brief introduction before looking at a key area of PPP activity—namely, their use by local governments for economic development or urban regeneration. Chapter Four investigates another major area, that of transportation, mainly roads, and more general infrastructure. Chapter Five looks at the important areas of health and education. Chapter Six aims to capture all the other areas which have been studied, but to a lesser extent, probably due to the much smaller amount of PPP activity within the various sectors. These include research and development (R&D) and other business initiatives, prisons, defence, waste management and water and to a lesser extent nuclear power and space exploration. This chapter will also look at research into contract management and accounting and finance issues. Chapter Seven outlines the methodology used in the study before presenting the results of the interviews with the key stakeholders. Chapter Eight will present four case studies of PPPs either under operation or in the planning stages in the USA. Chapter Nine draws on all the data gathered to make some comparisons between the two countries and also discusses the limitations of the study and ideas for future research.

2 Background to Public-Private Partnerships

Involving the private sector in the provision of public infrastructure projects such as schools, hospitals and roads is not a new idea. Indeed, the private sector will always have some input because in the majority of countries they are responsible for construction. However, following the macroeconomic dislocation of the 1970s and 1980s it was felt that some new thinking was required in order to address the poor state of the UK's public-sector infrastructure in the early 1990s. As a result of this the then Conservative Government introduced the PFI. Although there were to be many variations of this scheme, one of the most common forms of the PFI was the DBFO model. Under such an agreement the private sector would design and build the asset, arrange for its financing, provide maintenance over the life of the contract (normally 25–30 years) and also be responsible for the service provision. This latter facility depended on the type of asset being built; for example, in a PFI hospital the provision of medical care would still be provided by public-sector employees, whereas certain PFI prisons were run totally by private-sector personnel. The financing aspect is important as the public sector can borrow from Her Majesty's Treasurer (HMT), the lender of last resort, far cheaper than it can borrow from the private sector. This added cost is justified on the basis that the private sector needs to provide even greater efficiency savings and is generally seen to be taking on more of the risk.

In the first few years of the PFI only a small number of projects were signed and the UK private sector did not seem overly interested. One of the main reasons for this was that a private-sector contractor was expected to bear the risk if demand for the asset and associated service was less than expected. When the Labour party returned to power in 1997 they made several changes to the scheme, and, as well as not insisting that the private sector bear demand risk, they also changed the name of the scheme to the less controversial PPP. From 1997 onwards the amount of PPPs grew steadily, and up until the recent global financial crisis the average number of projects reaching financial close every year was 65, with a total value of £7.6 billion (HMT, 2003). In 2006 it was calculated that 641 projects worth just over £64 billion had been signed (HMT, 2006). However, despite a noticeable improvement in the UK's infrastructure and the other benefits they are seen to bring, PPPs have not been universally popular, particularly amongst academics.

The proponents of PPPs claim that they have a number of advantages over what was termed traditional procurement, where the private sector was completely responsible for only the building of infrastructure assets. Although a private company would have been involved in designing the asset, this was usually under clearly specified input instructions from the public-sector purchaser and separate companies would normally be involved in the design and construction phases. The proposed advantages include the fact that PPPs have been successful in attracting substantial private-sector finance, and it is possible to identify several large projects that probably would have been seriously delayed if they had not been financed by the private sector. These include the Channel Tunnel Railways Link and the Skye Bridge (National Audit Office (NAO), 1997). This argument is often tied to one of the original justifications for the initiative, which was it kept the UK government within prescribed borrowing limits. However, this led to a lengthy dispute about the correct accounting treatment of PPP assets, which will be dealt with in greater detail in Chapter Six.

Additionally, under traditional procurement there are separate design, construction, financing, operations and maintenance arrangements, whereas with PPPs (depending on the model adopted) they are combined under one contractor or a Special Purpose Vehicle (SPV). This integration or bundling provides financial motivation for the SPV to think beyond the design stage and build in features that may cost more initially but result in lower operating and running costs, and so deliver cost effectiveness over time (Grimsey and Lewis, 2004). Kee and Forrer (2008, p. 163) believe that 'in the political arena, little credit is given for long-range success. The political horizon is only as long as the next election. Thus, low cost bidding requirements may ignore life cycle cost issues, while change orders (sometimes the result of political pressures) drive up costs above original estimates'. Under traditional procurement, facilities were often under-maintained; faced with financial constraints a budget holder often took money for short-term concerns and neglected maintenance. For example, a principal of a school may have had to get in a temporary teacher to cover a sickness; as a result they would take money from the maintenance budget as it had no immediate significance. However, such actions can lead to much larger operational and even structural problems that cost more in the long term. This would not happen under a PPP as the maintenance budget is ring-fenced.

One of the key justifications for PPPs is that of risk transfer to the contractor, who is motivated to deliver the project within budget and on time as a result of the incentives offered to private companies through the payment mechanism. The NAO (2003a) reported that PPP projects had a much better track record than traditional procurement when it came to delivering construction projects on time. The allocation of risk is also seen to have benefits post-construction. If PPP contractors fail to perform operations or maintenance to the agreed standard they do not get paid, although this will be dependent on the contract. Finally, value for money (VFM) for the tax-payer is seen as another major justification for going down the PPP route. VFM is based on the idea that competitive tendering and superior private-sector efficiency can produce economies that offset both the higher cost of borrowing associated with some PPP models and the significant bidding costs. A study on behalf of the Commission on Public Private Partnerships by the Institute of Public Policy Research (IPPR) (2001) found cost savings of approximately 15% for PPP road and prison projects, with other proj-ects, such as school and hospital schemes, illustrating more marginal savings of approximately 2% to 4%. Another report by Arthur Andersen (2000) concluded that PPPs provided average cost savings of 17%.

There are a number of reasons why PPPs have been criticised, but a lot of the work in this area questions two of the major benefits outlined earlier: that they do not provide VFM and that sufficient risk is not being trans-ferred to the private sector. With regard to VFM, particularly in the case of hospitals, education and information technology (IT) projects, research has challenged the notion that PPP projects can deliver the anticipated VFM in the ways expected (see, for example, Gaffney and Pollock, 1999; Edwards and Shaoul, 2002, 2003). Moreover, some of the findings of the aforemen-tioned IPPR and Arthur Andersen reports have been questioned (see, respec-tively, Maltby, 2003; Ball et al., 2003a). Froud (2003) also feels that money that would have been recycled within the public sector is leaking out in the form of share dividends for investors. Rosenau (1999) also believes that evi-dence from the USA regarding cost efficiency is mixed. She considers the issue of externalities, which although important are seldom considered as they are 'so difficult to anticipate, to quantify, and to enter into any cost-benefit analy-sis of' PPPs (p. 14). She gives the example of workers who are employed at lower costs (e.g., lack of health insurance and other benefits), but could end up costing more to taxpayers as they make claims on government health and welfare benefits.

With regard to risk transfer there is the possibility that the contractor may not manage transferred risk effectively or the public sector may not have transferred the business risks that it believes it has. PPP contracts are rarely terminated, as essential public services must continue operating even if the contractor fails to deliver (see Brooks [2002] and Allen [2003] for examples of some PPP failures). Edwards et al. (2004), investigating PPP roads in the UK, believe that risk did not appear to have been transferred to the party best able to manage it. As a result the DBFO option has created additional costs and risks to the public agency, and to the public sector as a whole. Broadbent et al. (2008, p. 65) found that with regard to 17 PPP health projects when it came to performance measurement a 'considerable concentration of effort is addressed to the equivalent of only 43% of the total transferred risks. The other transferred risks and importantly those uncertainties that are to be shared are not addressed. This provides an important illustration of how certain items can be made invisible whilst others that are either deemed more significant or are possibly easier to monitor, are given unprecedented attention'. Furthermore, Pollock and Price (2008) highlighted that 'by October 2007, 622 PPP deals had been signed, (but) only 10 financial inquiries into central government operational PPPs had been undertaken by the NAO by 2006, and of these only three examined the relationship between risk transfer and risk premiums'; therefore, 'the government's central justification for PPP in terms of risk transfer remains largely unevaluated' (p. 176).

Another problem with PPPs is that they can be viewed as privatisation by the back door. One of the early arguments for PPP was it was seen as a method of bringing the benefits of privatisation to parts of the public sector, which, for either political or technical reasons, could not be straightforwardly privatised (Heald and Geaughan, 1997). However, there is often concern whenever the private sector gets involved in areas deemed to be under the control of the public sector, and this is normally connected with issues such as cost cutting impacting on service delivery and commercialisation. The particular unease regarding PPPs in the UK education sector is covered in more depth in Chapter Five. A related argument is sometimes referred to as 'cream skimming', when, for example, the private sector is interested only in running the better-quality schools (Levin, 1999) or insuring the healthiest patients (Sparer, 1999), thereby leaving the public sector to deal with the more problematic and expensive citizens. As Barker (1996) points out, as this means the public sector has to work in the more unprofitable areas of service provision, they are more likely to be labelled as inefficient.

The quality, design and innovation of PPP projects have also been called into question. The NAO (2003a) reported that there was a tendency for contractors to seek shortcuts in terms of quality of materials, finishing and general workmanship, if this could be achieved without prejudicing their income. The Commission for Architecture and the Built Environment (2002) identified deficiencies in the design of some early PPP schools, and similar concerns were expressed by the NAO. An evaluation of the Northern Ireland school Pathfinder projects concluded that there was limited innovation in terms of both design and service delivery (Northern Ireland Audit Office (NIAO), 2004). The major design problems cited were limited architectural contribution, together with poor specification, acoustics and visual environments. Moreover, two schools had almost identical design. It has also been highlighted that bundling may lead to a loss in operational efficiency, as the best developer is not necessarily the best operator (Laffont and Tirole, 1988). Furthermore, it may encourage choices that reduce future costs at the expense of service quality (Hart, 2003).

Rosenau (1999), writing in a US context, also looked at a number of other issues which she believes were disadvantages of PPPs. Firstly, could the higher costs of services provided by private partners lead to less democracy, access and equity for the users of these services? Secondly, a similar point is made about vulnerable populations who may be seen as expensive to service as they have increased needs. In such a case a private partner may try to seek savings in other ways. Love (1998) gives the example of private nursing homes that do not adequately screen staff and thus can end up employing workers with criminal records. Thirdly, PPPs do not necessarily lead to less regulation and thus an unintended, extra layer of bureaucracy can be created. Often the use of the private sector leads to more federal regulation (Sparer, 1999) and increased monitoring (Levin, 1999), the costs of which outweigh any savings. This increased regulation is also occurring in Europe (see, for example, Supiot, 1996; Saltman and Figueras, 1998). Fourthly, there are bound to be conflicts of interest between the shareholders of private companies involved in PPPs, who are seeking a good return, and the public-sector partners who want to see services provided to a higher standard and at a lower cost. Although it will be discussed in more detail in Chapter Six, a good example is private-sector prisons. The payment system encourages them to keep these prisons as full as possible, and thus the taxpayer could end up paying for people who do not necessarily need to be incarcerated (Schneider, 1999).

As a way of negating one of these potential drawbacks—the influence of shareholders—the non-profit distribution (NPD) model was introduced in Scotland. Although similar to a PPP, the main difference is that the NPD model provides economic or social infrastructure financed 100% by debt—90% senior and 10% junior. SPV shareholders receive a capped return on their capital, with any surpluses remaining at the end of the contract being passed to a designated charity as opposed to being paid out as dividends. Subsequently the dividend opportunity is removed, which is considered to flatten out overall risks when compared to equity-based PPPs or public procurement. NPD arrangements are therefore still attractive to banks, but not as popular with investors or bidders as they do not obtain the same returns (Hellowell and Pollock, 2009). The NPD is part of a wider initiative known as the Scottish Futures Trust (SFT), which has the aim of increasing VFM across all public-sector infrastructure investment (Scottish Futures Trust, 2011). The SFT is an arms-length government body that works with both the public and private sectors in order to drive down the costs of public procurement. As well as the NPD model, the SFT also uses a scheme known as tax incremental financing, whereby incremental tax revenues that arise from a procurement project are used to pay back the associated debt. This technique is one of a number that come under the umbrella of value capture in the USA (see Chapter Three for how tax incremental financing has been used and Chapters Eight and Nine for other value capture mechanisms).

In an attempt to increase VFM two other schemes were introduced in the UK, which aimed to take advantage of another form of bundling. These were the Local Improvement Finance Trust (LIFT) and Building Schools for the Future (BSF) initiatives. LIFT was introduced into the National Health Service (NHS) in order to create interest in small projects by bundling buildings together within a long-term partnership approach, which tied local

NHS organisations to a majority corporate-owned LIFT company (Aldred, 2008). Up until its introduction the main PPP focus had been on hospitals and not primary health care buildings. BSF took a similar approach, in that, instead of bidding to DBFO one school in a particular area, a bidder would save costs by tendering for a cluster of them. These savings would bring down the overall cost of the contract. Several drawbacks have been identified with the LIFT initiative (Aldred, 2008) and, due to what they saw as a huge waste of public money, the Coalition Government scrapped BSF in 2010 (BBC, 2010). However, this form of bidding for a cluster of schools has been used in the USA, albeit for managing them only (see Chapter Five).

To conclude, therefore, the amount of PPPs in the UK has continued to grow from their introduction in the early 1990s, and this rate of this growth has slowed only due to the start of the global financial crisis in 2008. However, since coming into power in 2010 the Coalition Government appears to have taken a more cautious approach to using PPPs as a means of further developing the UK's infrastructure. Whilst a number of reports from statutory bodies have been critical of PPPs, much greater criticism has come from UK academics who have very little positive to say about the scheme. Most of this criticism is down to a belief that PPPs do not provide the UK taxpayers with VFM and that insufficient risk has been transferred to the private sector. However, criticism of PPPs is also a feature of research in the USA. The next four chapters will look into PPP research in this latter country in much greater detail.

3 Public-Private Partnerships in the USA, Part I
Introduction, Local Authorities and Urban Regeneration

The use of PPPs is not restricted to the UK and variations of the DBFO model are utilised all over the world. For example, elsewhere in Europe countries making use of PPPs include Bulgaria, Croatia, the Czech Republic, Denmark, Finland, France, Germany, Greece, Hungary, Ireland, Italy, the Netherlands, Poland, Portugal, Romania, Slovenia and Spain. PPPs are also used in developed countries such as Australia, Canada and South Africa, countries that are witnessing rapid economic growth, namely China and India, and in some developing countries in both Africa and Asia. In the USA, whilst PPPs have been used for asset-based infrastructure projects—for example, toll roads and private prisons—they are also used for education policy priority setting, welfare provision, health and medical services and a range of community activities and services from schooling to urban regeneration and environmental policy (Grimsey and Lewis, 2004). When comparing the UK and USA, there are similarities when it comes to prisons, with the latter using the design, construct, maintain and finance model (very similar to DBFO), but differences when it comes to roads. According to Lockwood (1995) the three most common models of PPP for road building in the USA are BOO, BOT and build, transfer, operate (BTO), whereas in the UK it is mainly DBFO.

It is important to note that PPPs in the USA are nothing new and have been around for centuries. Indeed, Ewoh (2007, p. 360) points out that in '1652, the Boston Water Works Company was the first private corporation in this country to supply drinking water to citizens under (a) PPP contractual arrangement'. Further historical, more global examples of co-operation between the public and private sectors are provided by Hodge and Greve (2007, p. 545). Moreover, as Grimsey and Lewis (2005) indicate, the US market is fragmented and very diverse, with initiatives at the federal, state, local and municipal level. Additionally, unlike with other regions, there are no established procedures for risk transfer, risk valuation and establishing VFM, although in some cases, VFM is sought through the tendering process. This diverse nature of PPP markets may prove to be problematic when directly comparing countries with a more centralised decision making structure. However, the Coalition Government is aiming to devolve more powers to regional authorities and local governments; therefore the UK may be able to learn from how the various levels of governance in the USA manage PPPs. Interestingly Henderson and McGloin (2004) espoused the benefits of cross-border PPPs for both the Republic of Ireland and Northern Ireland, thereby suggesting a move away from regional arrangements.

Research into PPPs in the USA would be neither as extensive nor as critical as that of the UK; furthermore it reflects the more varied use of the scheme. A study into the number of PPP articles published in seven journals (mainly those connected to construction) between 1998 and 2008, conducted by Ke et al. (2009), found that out of 170 papers, 59 had originated from the UK (35%), whilst 25 (15%) had come from the USA. Whilst this is clearly a very selective sample it is probably an indicator of the difference between the two countries when it comes to PPPs as an area of academic interest. It is perhaps also noteworthy that these two countries were first and second in a table indicating the research origin of published PPP papers (p. 1079).

LOCAL AUTHORITIES AND URBAN REGENERATION

One area of great interest in the USA is PPPs between local authorities and private business, which have the aim of boosting economic development. Indeed, Hodge (2004) feels that PPPs in the USA have traditionally been associated with urban renewal and downtown economic development. Osborne (2001) states that PPPs have been central to national and state government initiatives to regenerate local urban communities, and have often arisen out of community-led attempts to deal with the crisis of government in US neighbourhoods. Wettenhall (2003, p. 83) feels that such initiatives can be traced back to the era of President Reagan, when there was a 'loosely bipartisan (Republican/Democrat) urging of a PPP effort to "save the cities"'. He also refers to and cites what he sees as a landmark book of the time written by Brooks et al. (1984). However, other writers feel that regeneration PPPs were first tried in the administration of President Carter in the late 1970s as local public officials searched for ways to advance redevelopment agendas in the context of declining federal revenues, double-digit inflation and growing anti-tax sentiment (for example, Frieden and Sagalyn, 1989; Sagalyn, 2007). Empirical studies have found that redevelopment PPPs are difficult to implement, limit opportunities for public participation and often fail to deliver citywide benefits (Sagalyn, 2007). Before looking specifically at urban regeneration PPPs, examples of other initiatives between the private sector and local government are provided.

Some work that looks at the role PPPs can play in local government in the USA has been conducted by Bloomfield (2006). She states that there were several challenges that long-term contracts between local government and private-sector organisations generated, and that these could undermine the successful implementation of such PPPs. These challenges were: a flawed competitive process that favours certain well-connected companies or consists of a limited pool of bidders; a lack of actual risk transfer; and a lack of transparency. A number of examples are provided of how the foregoing challenges led to PPPs that did not achieve the stated benefits of the scheme, such as improved service quality, risk sharing with the private sector, and cost savings. These include: a correctional facility in Plymouth County where, due to the limited competition, the private contractor was able to 'inflate their billings with fees for work that was not performed under contract and was not directly related to the project' (p. 402); a DBO contract for sewer construction in Lynn, Massachusetts, where in effect, and contrary to publicised claims, the contract assigned the risks of sewer overflows and flooding resulting from the contractor's redesign work to the public agency rather than to the contractor (Commonwealth of Massachusetts, Office of the Inspector General, 2001); and the aforementioned PPP in Plymouth County, where the taxpayers were unaware that they were going to pay for the entire project financing cost despite being assured (Renzi and Kelly, 1991) that the correctional facility was going to be built at no cost to them. The criticisms levelled at certain PPP contracts in this article have been well documented in UK research. For example, Pollitt (2000) highlights that most PPP projects have a small number of bidders, the lack of risk transfer has been widely covered (see, for example, Edwards et al., 2004; Hurst and Reeves, 2004; Lonsdale and Watson, 2007; Broadbent et al., 2008; Pollock and Price, 2008) and lack of transparency has been looked into by Hood et al. (2006). Likewise, the feeling that local government (and the public sector in general) need more expertise in order to deal with such complex contracts espoused by Bloomfield (2006) is an issue that has been subsequently looked at by the Organisation for Economic Co-operation and Development (OECD) (2008) and is addressed in Chapters Six, Seven and Nine.

Austin and McCaffrey (2002) looked at the role that business leaders played in PPPs associated with urban governance. They state that 'full-fledged governance regimes in American cities… . have tended to become even more rare' and that since the early 1980s there has been 'a proliferation of a heterogeneous variety of PPPs formed for a variety of purposes, including urban development, neighborhood rehab and betterment, or for special purpose projects' (p. 37). These business leaders tend to formally organise themselves into Business Leadership Coalitions (BLCs), and whilst BLCs can focus on issues of self-interest they also address 'quality of life issues' and work 'with city agencies or civic organisations to help make the community a better place to live and work' (p. 39). The authors found that sometimes these PPPs with BLCs come about due to some kind of fiscal or political crisis—for example, the New York and Boston BLCs formed due to actual or potential financial crises in those cities. Indeed, one of the key features of BLCs is their ability to raise money for public development purposes. However, the authors are keen to point out other key attributes business leaders bring to PPPs of this nature, such as entrepreneurial zeal, the ability to get things done and key links with the rest of the business community.

However, such PPPs did face challenges, which according to Austin and McCaffrey (2002) were both internal (e.g., disharmony) and external (e.g., changes to the political leadership of a city or a new generation of business leaders less concerned about civic values). They concluded that in order to survive, such PPPs needed to adapt and endure the challenging times that all cities face and changes to personnel, particularly chief executive officers (CEOs), of participating businesses.

Girard et al. (2009) investigated the role of PPPs in the delivery of municipal services in the predominantly rural area of New Hampshire. The focus was on the government of towns as opposed to large metropolitan areas. Similar, albeit mainly descriptive, work has also been conducted in towns in Illinois by Johnson and Walzer (1996) and Wisconsin by Deller at al. (2001). One particular problem with PPPs in small towns and rural areas appears to be the writing and enforcing of contracts. Many such towns are run by citizen volunteers and a small staff of employees (Honadle, 1983, 2001) with limited qualifications. As will be seen later in this book often large, well-staffed government departments find it hard to negotiate, monitor and enforce contracts; therefore 'the likelihood that smaller and rural local governments lack capacity to fully benefit from public-private partnerships is very high' (Girard et al., 2009, p. 374). The authors conducted a survey of 138 local town governments in New Hampshire and found that even the smallest municipalities were involved in some form of partnership with either non-profit or for-profit organisations. Those services whose contracts could be readily drafted and monitored tended to be outsourced the most, although some respondents were willing to look at other opportunities for contracting out. However, levels of satisfaction were fairly low for these outsourced services, possibly due to a significant proportion of the municipalities receiving insufficient bids (a common problem). Moreover, savings from these PPPs appeared to be fairly low and generally it was felt that privatisation required a trade-off between cost and quality. (This would be a common finding in the UK; see, for example, Northern Ireland Audit Office's (2004) review of the first six education projects in that country.) The chapter will now look at research that focuses on PPPs and urban regeneration.

A study that looks at the partnership between a region and the business community has been conducted by Detrick (1999), who looked at the role of PPPs in the redevelopment of Pittsburgh following the loss of the steel industry. The author highlights the fact that Pittsburgh has a long tradition of PPPs between government and business, with various arrangements going back as far as 1945. However, following the joint efforts of both the public and private sectors, the collapse of the steel and other manufacturing industries in the early 1980s did not lead to the expected huge rise in unemployment due to increases in other sectors, particularly the financial and services sectors. At the time the restructuring of both the region's economy and its partnership structures was hailed as a model of corporatist consensus in transforming the economic and social makeup of Pittsburgh (Ahlbrandt, 1990). However, in the 1990s both the strength of the region's economy and the partnership model weakened. Detrick (1999) thinks that, as the region's economic fortunes began to fade due to rising unemployment, the dominant partner in the Pittsburgh partnership model, the Allegheny Conference, reverted to top-down, corporate-based planning, leaving out much of the organised community and civic sectors that had gained strength over the two previous decades, and opted for business-led growth policies (Clavel and Kraushaar, 1998).

A more recent article looking at the role PPPs can play in the redevelopment of a region, in this case San Diego, has been written by Erie et al. (2010). Their research focuses on a PPP that linked construction of a downtown ballpark, Petco Park, to ancillary development in surrounding neighbourhoods. However, despite being heralded as a good example of the 'entrepreneurial approach to downtown redevelopment' in which cities are 'as focused upon the return on investment from the project as the private sector' (Chapin, 2002, pp. 565–566), the authors found that 'politics, not economics, was the driving force behind the Petco Park project and that private-sector actors have been the main beneficiaries' (Erie et al., 2010, p. 645). The three main reasons they give for the less than satisfactory outcome are all common criticisms of UK PPPs: information asymmetries and poor contract design during the formation of the PPP; flawed implementation of partnership agreements or their ex post renegotiation; and the failure of public officials to adequately monitor the performance of private partners.

The use of PPPs to build sports facilities has also been studied by Kennedy and Rosentraub (2000), who believe that most of these arrangements were very one-sided. 'In these partnerships, it is quite common for the public sector to be responsible for more than half of the construction costs while the teams retain the preponderance of revenues from ticket sales, luxury seating fees, concessions, advertising, (and) parking' (p. 437). Indeed, in an earlier study one of the authors had found that the public sector had actually assumed responsibility for 100% of the cost of a new stadium or arena whilst allowing teams to retain virtually all of the revenues generated by the new facility (Rosentraub, 1997). The reasons why governments invest so much were seen to be as follows: the intangible benefits of civic pride, community spirit and increased perceptions of quality of life generated by successful teams; and the hope that economic development and regional recreation patterns will be stimulated or redirected by the building of a new facility and a team's presence (Kennedy and Rosetraub, 2000). However, it would appear that economic development rarely materialises due to the presence of teams and the facilities they use. Moreover, if subsequent demands for more public funding from these teams are refused they often move on to other areas. The one-sidedness of this so-called partnership is further underscored by the benefits accrued to the team owners, who are able to use the extra revenues to substantially enhance the talent on the team (Rosentraub, 1998) and find that the value of the franchise has substantially increased if they sell their teams (Mullen, 1998; Zimbalist, 1998).

Consequently, Kennedy and Rosentraub (2000) set out 'to identify the tools available to the public sector to protect the long-term interests of tax-payers and governments that invest in facilities used by professional sports teams' (p. 438). They found that due to the powerful positions enjoyed by the teams, contracts and leases have little impact, and even when the public sector did successfully sue a team for a breach of contract, the damages were easily covered by the money it received from the community it moved to. The authors therefore suggested that the public sector should opt for a carefully crafted eminent domain statute. Eminent domain laws allow governments in the USA to lawfully take privately owned property for public purposes under certain conditions. In order for this to work the authors suggested certain policy and management issues must be addressed: the enabling legislation must identify the public purpose that is served by the presence of a professional sports team; the legislation developed must specify the tangible and intangible benefits anticipated from the team's presence and the investment of public funds in sports; states will generally need to pass an enabling law making it possible to condemn a team; the legislation permitting condemnation of a team should be enacted no later than the time the public subsidy is approved and preferably beforehand; and a process to evaluate and determine the fair or just compensation to be offered for a professional sports team needs to be considered. The authors concluded by stating that using eminent domain to protect a community's interests is not desirable and can be both costly and risky; 'but it may well be the only tool available as a result of the cartel of the major sports leagues and their inherent power to control the supply of teams' (p. 456).

Another study into economic development via PPPs in a specific region has been conducted by Ewoh (2007). His paper looks at the use of tax increment reinvestment zones (TIRZs) as a means of processing, financing and promoting PPPs in the City of Houston, Texas. Under an arrangement known as tax increment financing (TIF), a municipality will target a district for economic development and finance this development (via a private contractor) through property tax revenues generated from the growth in a district's assessed property values. The advantages of TIF are as follows: it is self-financing because it permits new development without reducing the city's total tax revenues; it provides substantial capital to allow economic development that would not have otherwise occurred; it restores the full tax base to all taxing jurisdictions once the project is completed and TIF bond paid off, which may increase the tax base for the affected local governments and reduce the local tax burden; and development initiated through its provision can serve as a catalyst for economic expansion by attracting more businesses and thus leading to an increase in the aggregate value of property both inside and outside the TIF area (Greuling, 1987; Man and Rosentraub, 1998). However, it has been argued that the incentives available through TIF are too inconsequential relative to the cost of production involved in the process (Byrne, 2005; Man and Rosentraub, 1998). Moreover, it can be viewed as a 'budget instrument adopted by municipalities to capture property tax revenue that would have gone to overlapping jurisdictions such as school districts, other special districts, and counties' (Ewoh, 2007, p. 362).

Despite these conflicting viewpoints, municipal officials in the USA still see TIF as a popular economic development tool. Indeed in December 2004, it was reported that 31 Texas cities had at least one TIRZ (Texas Comptroller of Public Accounts, 2004), with Houston having created 22 zones with TIF to fund developments. Ewoh's (2007) article looks at four of these TIRZs created in Houston, all of which were financially successful. Two of these had been initiated by the city, whilst the other two were established due to property owners within the zone filing a petition requesting the city to create them. However, he also highlighted one which had not been a success. This was a TIRZ created in 1997 to finance a high school in the Houston Independent School District. The only taxpayers in the zone (ExxonMobil, Texas Petrochemicals and Goodyear Tyre and Rubber Company) paid a combined tax liability of $129 million in 2005, which was less than half of what they paid in 1998. These companies reported huge profits but their commercial property values had not increased beyond their 1997 assessed value. Two factors are seen as contributing to the failure of this zone: the reduction in tax base revenue was due to an economic slump in the oil industry, which affected business activities; and the three companies' tax protests pressured the Harris County Appraisal District to reduce their tax liability. Because commercial property tax is not tied to corporate financial performance, some citizens were not pleased that the school district was forced to absorb the payment of nearly $100 million for the high school construction (Castro and Stillman, 2005). Ewoh (2007) states that the lesson to be learned from this TIRZ's financial problem was that a new zone should not be created without a sustainable tax base to generate enough tax increment revenue in order to meet its obligation. As stated in Chapter Two, TIF is one of several techniques that have been collectively labelled as value capture; this will be looked at in more detail in Chapters Eight and Nine.

Examples where PPPs have been used for financing federal capital, which is subsequently used for spending on land improvements and buildings, are provided by Gallay (2006). He states that such PPPs are rare and are used by federal agencies as one of an array of approaches for obtaining capital without seeking specific budget authority. Proponents of PPPs of this nature argue that they provide a federal agency with a realistic alternative for obtaining capital that is less costly than the normal budgeting process. From a federal agency's perspective, such partnerships can be very attractive because it can obtain capital without first having to secure sufficient budget appropriations to cover the full cost of the capital. However, critics of these ventures caution that they are not the least expensive means of meeting capital needs, although they may appear to be in the short term (US General

Accounting Office (GAO), 2003). The examples he highlights are the US Postal Service, which leased some of its land to the city of New Brunswick, New Jersey, in return for the renovation of the city's main post office; the Veteran Affairs Administration, which leased an underused medical centre to a private developer, who in turn built an office building for Veterans Affairs; and the Department of Energy, which sold unneeded land at its Oak Ridge National Laboratory to a private developer, who in turn built a building and leased it to the department's prime contractor for Department of Energy mission support. These are all examples of the private sector leveraging public-sector assets, and this subject will be looked at in more detail in Chapters Eight and Nine. In his paper, Gallay (2006) uses a hypothetical situation in order to test the validity of such a use of a PPP. He concludes that the present value of the costs to the federal agency for pursuing the PPP during the 25-year period is roughly the same as if it acquired the building itself with budget authority; however, with a PPP, the agency would be able to meet its facility needs at least two years earlier at no additional cost. He therefore believes that PPPs 'can be a useful technique for federal agencies to acquire federal capital' (p. 150).

Another interesting study on finance as a means of redeveloping an area has been conducted by Rubin and Stankiewicz (2001). Their paper looks at the formation of the Los Angeles Community Development Bank (LACDB) in 1995 via a PPP consisting of city and county officials, private business and the local community. This was in response to the Los Angeles riots of 1992, and the aim was to set up a non-profit institution that would help stimulate investment and create jobs in the city's riot-scarred areas and other poor communities. Lending facilities were to be provided by both the government and four regional commercial banks. Despite being greeted with great enthusiasm and expectation, by 2000 the LACDB was facing an uncertain future with satellite branches having closed, half of its staff laid off and the majority of lending curtailed. This was due to a 32% loan default rate, a failure to meet its job creation targets and a high number of lawsuits from borrowers. According to the authors, LACDB encountered a number of problems, some of which could have been avoided during the planning process. It found itself competing unfavourably with the federal Small Business Administration, who lent at more favourable terms than it did, plus as the economy improved the aforementioned four commercial banks began to 'cherry-pick' the more profitable deals in the bank's geographical area (LACDB, 1999). Moreover, the high cost of capital for LACDB meant that it was actually losing money on each loan it made, even if these loans were fully repaid. Part of the problem according to the authors was that the LACDB was not a true partnership, with the four private banks neither involved in a long-term relationship with the bank, nor having a shared responsibility for its outcomes. Other problems were: there was too much faith in business practices; the PPP emphasised packaging and marketing rather than systemic change; as is common with other PPPs the partnership with the private sector brought with it conflicts of interest and cost shifting (i.e., LACDB was left with the more expensive clients); and the PPP led to both a decrease in accountability and a less efficient organisation. Despite some optimism by the authors towards the end of the paper, the bank finally did close in March 2004 due to insolvency (Krol and Svorny, 2004).

Finally, Wilkey (2000) outlines the work done in the area of urban regeneration by the Argonne National Laboratory, in Argonne, Illinois. The paper is more of an overview of what the organisation is capable of—for example, helping industries operate more efficiently with regard to energy consumption and environmental emissions and industrial redevelopment, rather than focusing on any specific PPPs. Moreover it sees its role as a coordinator and facilitator of any relevant PPP, as it aims to bring together a variety of technical expertise, from both the public and private sectors, in order to propose, develop and execute strategies for addressing the various needs of urban industrial areas.

CONCLUSIONS

PPPs have been used for a wide range of activities in both the provision of services that would normally come under the remit of local government and boosting the economy of a region. However, despite some successes with TIRZs, which benefit from an increase in property tax revenues, and BLCs, which can help a region get out of a financial crisis, most of the research seems to focus on PPP projects that either were flawed from the outset or initially seemed to be performing beneficially before the private partners began to behave in more of an opportunistic manner. Problems that have dogged UK projects are highlighted in many of the initiatives reviewed—for example, a flawed competitive process with a small pool of private bidders; a lack of risk transfer; a lack of transparency; low levels of satisfaction for outsourced services; a trade-off between cost and quality; poor contract design; inadequate monitoring by public-sector officials; and a partnership weighted in favour of the private partner. Urban regeneration will be looked at again in Chapters Seven, Eight and Nine. The next chapter looks at another major area of PPP activity in the USA—namely, transportation and infrastructure.

4 Public-Private Partnerships in the USA, Part II

Transportation and Infrastructure

There are always fears when the private sector becomes involved in road building, particularly when their upfront and ongoing costs are recaptured by tolls. It is felt that PPPs of this nature 'will lead to increased costs for users and the possible exclusion of those who cannot afford to pay tolls, sometimes on roads that had previously been toll free' (Ortiz and Buxbaum, 2008, p. 127). These authors state that public concerns regarding such contracts could be divided into three areas: aspects of public-sector decision-making; conflicts between private-sector and public-sector interests; and contract terms and how they affect price and public control. They also believe that although PPPs can bring with them many cost-saving features, this does not mean that the public sector does not have other means of achieving some or all of the benefits. In the UK, where many early PPPs were transport-oriented, Edwards et al. (2004) examined the first eight DBFO road projects in England and are highly critical regarding issues such as VFM and risk transfer. Clearly infrastructure refers to more than just road building, and other projects that are relevant to this term will be covered in this chapter; however, the majority of research is concerned with roads.

TRANSPORTATION AND INFRASTRUCTURE

As in other countries, PPPs were used in the USA as a tool to fill the funding gap for infrastructure development. Reports from the Federal Highway Administration (FHwA) (see, for example, FHwA, 2004) projected serious shortfalls between federal, state and local highway revenues and the investment requirements needed to maintain and improve the highway facilities. The use of PPPs to bridge this gap has been promoted since 1991, following the passing of a number of acts, which were intended 'to encourage private sector participation in highway infrastructure projects and to provide project financing opportunities to the states' (Abdel Aziz, 2007, p. 919). In order to further promote and standardise PPP procurement practices, the American Bar Association (2000) developed a model procurement code and the FHwA (2007) produced a working draft of PPP legislation for states to consider when developing their own legislation.

Table 4.1   Sponsors and Features of Highway Financing in the USA (Engel et al., 2006)

Sponsor	Major Features of Financing	Examples
Private equity investors	Finance and develop the project using private resources	Dulles Greenway (Virginia); 91 Express Lane project (California)
Private, non-profit entity	Issues tax-exempt debt backed by tolls (and without recourse to taxes) and oversees the project under the terms of the agreement between the state and the private developer	TH (Trunk Highway) 212 (Minnesota); Southern Connector (South Carolina); Interstate 985 (Virginia); Tacoma Narrows Bridge (Washington); Arizona toll projects
Special-purpose public agency	Issues tax-exempt debt backed by tolls (and without recourse to taxes) and oversees the project under the terms of the agreement with a private developer	E (Expressway)–470 (Colorado); Orange County, California, transportation corridor agencies
State agency	Issues tax-exempt debt backed by tolls and without recourse to taxes	Some turnpikes
State agency	Issues tax-exempt debt backed by taxes	Most highway projects that are financed by debt
State agency	Finances highway on a pay-as-you-go basis using state taxes and fees plus federal aid	Most highways

As a result of these and other efforts $41.5 billion worth of PPP road projects were executed between 1985 and 2004. Alongside the various arrangements (see Table 4.1) tolls were imposed on existing high occupancy highway lanes and existing highway assets were sold. For example, in 2005, the Chicago Skyway was sold for $1.8 billion (see Levy [2008] and Ortiz and Buxbaum [2008] for fuller descriptions of this PPP and a similar deal in Indiana). According to FHwA (2006) and Reason Foundation (2006), the proceeds from the tolls and asset sales were used by a number of states to raise funds needed for road repairs and expansion, adding new roads and relieving congestion. However, despite these initiatives, the implementation of PPPs in the USA has been facing difficulties. These include: a lack of relevant state laws and policies; a lack or discontinuity of public-sector leadership; a satisfaction with traditional procurement; opposition from the local community and transportation programme administrators/staff;

Table 4.2 Regional Share of PPP Projects Funded and Completed between 1985 and 2004 (Adapted by Abdel Aziz, 2007 from FHwA, 2005a)

Region	Percentage (%)
Europe	37.8
Asia and the Far East	36.7
North America	15.8
Latin America, Africa, Middle East	9.7
Total ($450.9 billion)	100

lack of familiarity with the mechanisms for developing and implementing PPP projects; bureaucratic government processes for environmental review, right-of-way acquisitions and project contracting; cultural differences between the public- and private-sector interests; and lack of dedicated revenue sources/innovative financing tools to enable projects to be developed (FHwA, 2005b). With regard to state laws, FHwA reported in 2006 that out of 52 states and territories, only 22 states (including one territory) had PPP-enabling acts; however, some acts were enabled only for pilot and demonstration projects, and some of the states' acts (five out of 22) put restrictions on the geographic location of the PPP project, whereas other states (11 out of 22) had restrictions on the type of transportation mode eligible for PPP delivery. (For more up-to-date figures see Istrate and Puentes, 2011.) A survey conducted by Papajohn et al. (2011) found that: ten states were either experienced with, or currently practicing, transportation PPPs; 15 had plans to implement them; and seven did not plan to implement them. According to the authors the states in this latter category tend to be located towards the north central and western part of the USA and have not yet planned to implement PPPs primarily owing to relatively low traffic volume. Moreover, states with PPP experience tend to have legislation that is favourable toward PPPs. It should be noted that 18 states did not respond to their survey.

Abdel Aziz (2007) states that North America's (which includes Canada) implementation of PPPs for roads has been less extensive that that of other regions and the design and build (DB) / design, build, operate and maintain (DBOM) arrangements have been highly preferred to the BOT/BTO/concession arrangements. A DB project is where a single private partner designs and constructs a facility, which 'has the advantage of allowing one firm to use its information, knowledge, and skill to coordinate a facility's design with its construction' (Geddes, 2011, p. 29). This is distinct from a Design Bid Build contract, which is where different contractors design and build the asset and is another name for traditional procurement. Abdel Aziz adopted two tables in order to show the varying degrees of usage, of both PPPs and

Table 4.3   Regional Distribution of PPP Arrangements for Road Projects between 1985 and 2004 (Adapted by Abdel Aziz, 2007 from FHwA, 2005a)

Region	BOT/BTO/Concession	DBFO	DBOM/DB
Europe	44.6	58.1	31.9
Asia and the Far East	27.2	31.1	20.3
North America	16	3.5	43.6
Latin America, Africa, Middle East	12.2	7.3	4.2
Total ($322.4 billion)	100	100	100

types of PPPs, by countries worldwide (see Tables 4.2 and 4.3). It should be noted that both of these tables refer to PPP road projects only.

Engel et al. (2006) reviewed two private toll roads built using a BOT arrangement during the 1990s, specifically the Dulles Greenway Highway and the California Orange County State Route 91 (SR 91) express lanes. The former proved problematic for the investors due to an underestimation of how much users dislike paying tolls. Furthermore, the State of Virginia subsequently widened the toll-free road the Greenway Highway was meant to relieve, therefore negating demand. Vining et al. (2005, p. 206) state that this PPP illustrated 'a "vicious cycle" that seems to afflict quite a few highway projects: tolls are set high in an attempt to cover financing and operating costs, demand is overestimated at that toll, the toll discourages usage and thus total revenues are not high enough to cover financing and operating costs. Tolls are lowered, as a result demand increases, but total revenues do not increase substantially and still do not cover financing and operating costs; the builder/ operator requests some form of bailout by government and if it does not get it the firm slides into technical default'. The opposite problem occurred with the SR 91 express lanes (Engel et al., 2006), where demand got so great despite several increases in the toll that congestion occurred at peak times. However, due to clauses in the contract, the contractor was not allowed to widen the highway and therefore was unable to maximise revenue. Vining et al. (2005) outline the various attempts taken by both main partners to circumvent this problem and the eventual sale of SR 91 back to the government. They conclude that although this PPP was successful with regard to the cost of construction, quality and usage, both 'parties exhibited opportunistic behavior and the transaction costs, including legal costs and negotiation costs, were enormous' (p. 207). (For a further discussion of the SR 91 PPP, see Siemiatycki, 2010.) Engel et al. (2006) believe that in both cases a present-value-of-revenue (PVR) auction would have solved the different sets of problems faced by the respective contractors, as it reduces risk and can make it easier to change the terms of the contract.

PVR-type contracts have been used in the UK (the Queen Elizabeth II Bridge on the River Thames and the second Severn bridges on the Severn Estuary) and Chile (a major improvement of the highway joining the capital, Santiago, and the seaport of Valparaiso). They work in the following way. Concessionaires bid on the basis of the lowest present value of toll revenue they will accept from a PPP project. The franchise for the winning bidder then comes to an end when the toll revenue received equals the amount they bid. One major advantage of this type of auction is that it eliminates demand risk for the private partner. If traffic is lower than expected, then the franchise simply lasts longer (Engel et al., 2001). Thus the risk premium demanded by firms is lower than those for fixed-term concessions, which should attract investors at lower interest rates (Engel et al., 2011). A further advantage of a PVR contract is that it is easier to buy back the project if it becomes necessary to do so. The uncollected revenue (minus reasonable expenses for operations and maintenance) provides a fair compensation, which is a far more straightforward compensation mechanism for a possible buyback than those for other award options (Engel et al., 2011).

There are various ways of paying for roads, apart from tolls, and this has formed the basis of some research. For example, in states such as Massachusetts and New Mexico, PPPs are supported by state bonds for major highway expansions (National Council for Public-Private Partnerships (NCPPP), 2002; Walton and Euritt, 1990). More recently a PPP based on shadow tolls has been used in the El Paso Inner Loop Project in Texas. This is a method popular in the UK, whereby government pays the toll instead of the motorist, with 'payments based upon assumed traffic volume and the level of service that is expected from the project's operator' (Levy, 2008, p. 225). Another arrangement used in PPP road building is that of availability payments. Under such a scheme the public sector pays a private company for the provision of road services, withholding payment only if the road becomes unavailable. This could occur if the road was not maintained properly or if there was insufficient traffic management following an accident. Such a method is being used in the Port of Miami Tunnel Project (Levy, 2008). For descriptions of other road PPP projects see Ortiz and Buxbaum (2008), who have looked at a number of deals including two others in Texas (Trans Texas Corridor 35 and State Highway 130) and the Pennsylvania Turnpike. As will be seen in Chapter Seven, this latter PPP deal did not eventually materialise due to political delays.

A more specific piece of research into the use of PPPs in transportation comes from Battaglio and Khankarli (2008) with their study of Texas State Highway 121. The article looks at the objection of the local community to a Spanish private company being awarded the PPP contract for the reconstruction of the aforementioned road and the subsequent tolling, which led to a public-public partnership being formed with a local toll-road authority. The authors state that as 'opposition to the toll road grew among a public concerned with foreign involvement in the undertaking and the negative perception of business motives, political and administrative institutions were forced into action to ameliorate the accountability gap by' amending existing legislation (p. 145). Their research underlines the important role that public sentiment can play in political decisions, especially when accountability is at stake. This area of accountability has been further investigated in the USA by Forrer et al. (2010), who state that it needed to be improved in order maintain public trust in government, and uphold the public interest through multi-sector delivery of public services. The authors propose a PPP accountability framework, which consists of six dimensions: risk; cost and benefits; social and political impact; expertise; partnership collaboration; and performance measurement. Work on a public framework of accountability has also been conducted by Minow (2003), who states that governments who contracted services to a private-sector provider, either via PPPs or other arrangements, should still be 'held responsible for consequences resulting from such contracts' (p. 1260). Levy (2008) states it is important to ask why so many foreign developers are coming to the USA and bidding for infrastructure projects, believing that it is because they gained experience in similar projects in Europe, Asia and South America. Therefore, it is necessary for lenders, designers and contractors in the USA to gain a similar experience domestically so they can compete on a global scale. There are two noteworthy points from the work of Battaglio and Khankarli (2008); firstly the mistrust of foreign involvement in PPPs and secondly the impact that public opposition can have. These subjects will be looked at again in Chapters Seven and Nine.

Other research has justified the use of the private sector in road building. For example, in a study on highway PPPs in the USA, Poole (2006) ascertained that government-run toll roads had not raised tolls on two of the projects studied for 20 and 12 years, respectively. As a result, needed investment was not made. Transferring those roads to a PPP, where toll rates are set by the market, can capture value and fund further investment. As the study noted, the shift of control to a non-political entity that is capable of behaving over time in an economically rational manner opens up financial possibilities that depend on the financial markets' recognition of that reality. Garvin (2010) looked at the role of PPPs in transportation after the financial crisis of 2008–2009. He states that the PPP market in the USA was fairly stagnant, therefore sharing similarities with the UK, where the number of projects coming to a financial close has reduced drastically (see Connolly and Wall, 2011). However, he states that in the USA 'they will not vanish from the transportation infrastructure provision tool kit' (Garvin, 2010, p. 402). He cites the recent example of Florida's Interstate (I)-595 Express project, where well over half of the funding required was provided by bank loans ($780 million) and equity ($190 million), which was a positive sign that the capital markets will support strong projects (Halai, 2009). Indeed, as will be seen in Chapters Seven to Nine, private finance of transportation projects is being actively encouraged in the USA during the economic downturn.

Finally with regard to roads, Zhang (2004) discusses how the South Carolina Department of Transportation (SCDOT) used a unique technique for evaluating tenders for four BOT-type toll roads in California—these being the Santa Ana Viaduct Express, Mid-State Tollway, San Miguel Mountain Parkway and the aforementioned SR 91. The results of the tender evaluation are represented by four charts. The first, a value chart, displays each tender's scope of work, total project costs, right-of-way acquisition process, maintenance, law enforcement provisions and toll collection policies. The second chart lists each tender's source of revenue, funding required from revenue bonds, toll collections, state obligation bonds and investment earnings. The third chart compares cash outlays of each tender. The fourth chart addresses financial risks by rating each tender's financial plan dependency in one of four categories: high, medium, medium-high and very high. An overview tabulation would then be prepared, based on which SCDOT finally determined and then began negotiations with the preferred bidder (Levy, 1996).

Another interesting piece of research regarding PPPs in transportation was conducted by Dunn in 1999. He states that two broad categories can be identified: policy-level partnerships and project-based partnerships. It could be argued that the former is nothing more than the normal interaction of government and business—for example, capping prices of private-sector providers of rail services or imposing a tax on fuel in order to try to reduce the use of motor vehicles. The author points out that such partnerships are not new and one could go back to the Federal Aid Road Act of 1916 and the Federal Aid Highway Act of 1921, which laid the foundations of a policy-level partnership that explicitly linked federal and state governments and implicitly included important sections of the business community as well as millions of individuals (Seely, 1987). However, the latter includes schemes that would normally come under the umbrella of PPPs—for example, encouraging private business to invest in transport infrastructure projects such as the aforementioned SR 91 in California's Orange County. A different type of project-based partnership was the Partnership for a New Generation of Vehicles that was set up in 1993 by the Clinton administration and the Big Three automobile companies based in Detroit (i.e., General Motors, Ford and Chrysler). This partnership had the aim of creating a joint research programme 'to develop a passenger vehicle that was three times more fuel efficient than a 1994 intermediate size car by the year 2004' (Dunn, 1999, p. 97). The author states that as the motor vehicle remains the most popular means of travel, a PPP of this nature was more likely to succeed than one that tried to encourage people to use more public transport. Indeed, this PPP has been successful and is ongoing at the time of writing. However, one consequence of more efficient vehicles has been less revenue gained via fuel tax in the USA; this will be further discussed in Chapter Eight.

Work that spans the boundary of both transport and IT with regard to PPPs has been conducted by Lawther (2004, 2005), who looked at the development of Advanced Traveller Information Systems (ATIS) that communicate information about traffic congestion to the travelling public in a timely manner. It is felt that ATIS might significantly help to lessen traffic congestion and thereby reduce both travel times and traffic fatalities. Moreover, the 'effective deployment of ATIS infrastructure components or subsystems requires cooperation and coordination among public sector agencies, from whom data regarding transportation conditions are collected, and among private contractors who often provide needed expertise and deployment capabilities' (2005, p. 1118). Such PPPs have been in existence since 1996 and have gone through several changes since that time. One early problem was that in many metropolitan areas private partners were unable to sell advertising and individualised subscriptions as expected (Schuman and Sherer, 2001), which resulted in public partners not being able to share any generated revenue. Moreover, technology advancements have changed the nature of the PPPs, involving a greater number of local transportation and law enforcement agencies and providing greater amounts of data to be processed.

Generally, Lawther (2005, p. 1122) believes that 'even though there have been few PPP successes in providing ATIS, the potential benefits outweigh the potential risks'. He subsequently suggests five different partnership models for ATIS, giving examples of existing arrangements in each. The five models are: public controlled; public stimulated and funded; public stimulated but not funded; private partnered; and private controlled. These in effect go along a continuum from maximum to minimum public-sector control, and it could be argued that those at either end are not really PPPs at all. Under the public controlled model, data exchange is limited or nonexistent, and with the private controlled model, the private partner controls the revenue generated and the amount returned to the public partners. Public stimulated and funded indicates that the main duty of the private partner is the dissemination of traffic data. The main difference between public stimulated but not funded and private partnered is funding. With the former model it is hoped that the dissemination of private-sector information can be stimulated without public support and resources, whereas with the latter the public partner pays the private one to provide all functions. The author concludes that for these types of PPPs to be successful there needs to be: technology of a sufficient quality; effective dissemination of accurate data; and strong marketing efforts on behalf of the private partners in order to attract subscribers and advertisers.

In his earlier paper, Lawther (2004) states that the public partner also has a marketing role to play, which is convincing the travelling public to use the information provided by the ATIS. He also outlines some of the risks to the public partner in entering such a PPP. These are: the travelling public may feel that building more roads is more appropriate than technological solutions when it comes to reducing traffic congestion; the service offered by the private partners will fail to be accepted by enough consumers, resulting in them going bankrupt; and that the ATIS deployment may fail due to the travelling public not being aware of its existence, not using it or not believing it is achieving its aim of reducing congestion. At the time the article was written, the general awareness levels of ATIS were low despite the large numbers of them deployed across the USA. Lawther goes on to give three examples of how public outreach efforts have generally been unsuccessful. In the first of these, the AZTech ATIS PPP in the Phoenix Metropolitan Area, three groups were targeted as part of the public outreach campaign: stakeholders, media representatives and the travelling public. However, the 'AZTech plan focused more on increasing and maintaining stakeholder support rather than on generating public awareness and usage' (p. 126). In Washington, District of Columbia (DC), a PPP known as Partners in Motion eventually failed despite a comprehensive public outreach campaign; this was partly attributed to a less than optimal coordination of efforts. The public outreach campaign in the third case study, the South Florida SUNGUIDE ATIS PPP, was given a high priority and used a variety of marketing techniques. Despite these efforts the overall campaign was not successful, and the author suggests that this could be due to other marketing opportunities being missed. One solution to this lack of awareness of ATIS has been to provide more consistency nationwide for telephone advisory services, with the US Department of Transportation (USDOT) petitioning the Federal Communications Commission to assign 511 as the nationwide telephone number for traveller information in July 2000 (USDOT, 2000).

PPPs that come under the broader umbrella of infrastructure have been looked at by Daniel (2008), who feels that they 'not only are desirable but are vital to sustaining quality infrastructure' (p. 89). He divides expectations regarding infrastructure into six categories, feeling that strong PPPs are the only way that these can be achieved. These categories are: the ability to move people and things (e.g., water, electricity, goods and information); quality of life; reliability; safety; cost (i.e., coping with the trade-off between minimum expenditure and maximum value); and protection of the homeland. He uses the example of the devastation caused to New Orleans by Hurricane Katrina to highlight how PPPs could have prevented the extent of damage and disruption, citing clear lines of authority and a focus on factors that are truly critical as issues that PPPs can address.

Finally, a PPP that was utilised to rebuild Washington, DC's Union Station used no incremental taxpayer money at all. According to the NCPPP (2005), the private-sector partner recouped its costs in part from rents paid by retail shops in the renovated facility. This is a good example of a truly innovative PPP, which although needing regulatory and legislative approval, required little or no public money. Therefore, the normal argument that the cost of PPPs can end up being higher is not applicable in this case. Examples of PPPs in the actual 'railroad industry include the Alameda Corridor (Long Beach to Los Angeles), the Chicago Region Environmental and Transportation Efficiency Program, the Heartland Corridor (the East Coast to Chicago), the Reno Trench, and the New Orleans Gateway' (Papajohn et al.,

2011, p. 132). The Union Station PPP is returned to in Chapter Eight as one of the case studies.

CONCLUSIONS

The increasing use of the motor car as a means of transport has led to demands for more road building to ease congestion and improve journey times, particularly for those travelling to and from work. Moreover, increasing usage means that roads have to be maintained and repaired more often. This demand cannot be met from the public purse only; however, whilst it may seem practical to fill any funding gap by involving the private sector, such arrangements are not without their problems. A common way for a private-sector operator to recoup its costs is via tolling, yet many citizens object to paying for something that was hitherto free of charge. Furthermore, if a private company finds that it is not breaking even, or making a suitable return for its shareholders, it could be tempted to increase the toll charges, thereby forcing some users out of the market. Nonetheless, a large number of PPP projects have been initiated since 1985, although with mixed success. The Dulles Greenway Highway project suffered from a lack of users, whilst the SR 91 express lanes in California experienced such high demand that congestion still occurred at peak times. In Texas, local opposition was so great that plans to award a contract for a highway to a Spanish company were abandoned and instead a public-public partnership was formed.

More equitable PPPs from the perspective of the motorist are those financed by shadow tolls, in which the government effectively pays, and those subject to availability payments, in which the private contractor gets paid only if the road is available. Research has also shown that the private sector is more effective at setting toll rates and that revenue received can lead to greater investment in this sector. However, not all of the research focussed specifically on roads, with some interest shown in the mainly unsuccessful attempts to use PPPs to provide the travelling public with up-to-date traffic information via IT. Such partnerships appeared to have failed due to sub-optimal marketing campaigns. A far more successful, and longstanding, PPP concerns a project between government and the major automobile companies to produce more fuel-efficient and environmentally friendly vehicles. However, as will be seen in Chapter Eight more fuel efficiency is one of a number of factors that has led to less fuel tax being collected. Less work has looked at other types of infrastructure PPP projects, although the rebuilding of Washington, DC's Union Station provides a good example of innovative financing arrangements. Transportation is one of the main areas covered in Chapter Seven and provides the basis for all four case studies in Chapter Eight.

5   Public-Private Partnerships in the USA, Part III
Health and Education

This chapter will look at two of the most important areas of public service delivery, health and education. In the UK any attempt by governments to involve the private sector in either area is met with suspicion and hostility. However, in the USA there has traditionally been much greater involvement by private companies in health provision, although PPPs are not generally used for hospital building in that country. As will be seen, however, some writers have been critical of private-sector involvement in US schools, and thus there is more common ground between the two academic communities with regard to the use of PPPs in education.

HEALTH

PPPs in health are an area of great controversy in the UK, particularly with regard to projects involving the building of hospitals. A number of articles have criticised their use in the NHS, with the main thrust of the arguments provided being that not only do PPPs fail to give VFM, but they also impact on the care of patients. For example, Gaffney et al. (1999) state that the bulk of risk in a PPP hospital was transferred to the building period—i.e., the first three to five years—rather than to the operational phase—i.e., the subsequent 25–30 years. In effect this meant that during this latter phase risks were transferred on 'spurious grounds', in that although risks were apparently transferred to private-sector companies they faced no financial penalties if they failed to achieve targets. Barnett (1999) echoes the sentiments of many academics and NHS personnel when he reports that hospitals built under the PPP initiative were ending up with fewer beds, which inevitably meant cuts in personnel. Mayston (1999, p. 250) states that NHS decision makers had a 'lack of freedom' when it came to choosing between publicly and privately provided new capital assets because the available funds for direct capital expenditure in the NHS were being reduced 'with PFI schemes being the only permitted way of funding the short-fall'. He sees it as a short-term solution that will be ultimately paid for by future taxpayers. For similar arguments and criticisms see Boyle, 1997; Gaffney and Pollock, 1999; Pollock et al., 1999, 2000, 2002; Broadbent et al., 2008; Shaoul et al., 2008.

However, there is a much larger private-sector involvement in the USA, with it being the largest employer of health care providers and with private health insurers paying for most of the country's health care bill (Sparer, 1999). This private-sector involvement is a mixture of not-for-profit and for-profit organisations, with a higher percentage of the former. Whilst the author has tried to limit the subsequent review to PPPs consisting of for-profit organisations only, it is possible that some of the companies mentioned are not-for-profits. However, the comments regarding not-for-profit organisations in the health sector by one of the interviewees in Chapter Seven highlight that these organisations are still seeking a healthy surplus of income over expenditure. It should also be noted that hospital building via PPPs does not generally take place in the USA. A rare example is the building of the Veterans Affairs Medical Centre Complex in Durham, North Carolina, which took place in the late 1990s (Stainback, 2000). Therefore, research has focussed on other areas. For example, Awofeso (2007) discussed the contentious issue of private prison health care contracts in the USA, where prison health care privatisation was at the time a $2-billion-a-year industry. As early as 2000, 34 states had some privatised health care for prisoners, whilst the inmate health care systems of 24 states were run completely by private contractors. Proponents of privatisation argue that by allowing competition for prison health services, policymakers can cut costs and improve quality at all levels of the correctional health care system (Montague, 2003). However, its opponents, including most prisoner advocacy groups, argue that the savings from prison health privatisation are usually due to swingeing cuts to inmates' medical services and staff salaries. Moreover, many of the large private correctional health care providers in the USA, such as Prison Health Services, Inc., face a growing list of lawsuits from prisoners who allege deliberate disregard for their health needs (von Zielbauer, 2007).

The broader area of health has received a great deal of interest in the USA. Bazzoli et al. (1997) looked at PPPs that join two types of networks that collaborate on health and human service delivery. These were local coalitions of public and private stakeholders that focus on public health and community planning, and service delivery networks that seek to co-ordinate and provide collaboratively a continuum of services. The authors found that there was extensive collaborative action when it came to identifying and evaluating community health needs, a certain amount of collaboration in assisting individuals in obtaining services from multiple providers and in reporting information to the community, and limited collaboration in reducing redundancies and increasing efficiencies. It was felt that such PPPs held great potential for both improving community health and enhancing the co-ordination and effectiveness of local health delivery. Another article by Crowley et al. (2004) proposes the establishment of a unique PPP called the National Clinical Research Enterprise, which should have an agenda of: informed public participation; supportive information technologies; a skilled workforce; and adequate funding in clinical research. The authors state that clinical research in the USA is at a critical crossroads, and that it needs to be transformed from a cottage industry to an enterprise-wide health care pipeline with the function of bringing novel research from both government and private entities to the American public.

Another area in which PPPs are seen to be effective is that of tobacco control. Houston (2002) discusses several successful projects in the USA. For example, in 1991, the National Cancer Institute's American Stop Smoking Intervention Study (ASSIST) was implemented as a prevention and tobacco use reduction strategy. Interventions in 17 states across the USA included the development of both state-wide and local coalitions that brought together state and local public health departments, the American Cancer Society state divisions and local units, and a variety of other private-sector groups involved in tobacco control. ASSIST's comprehensive programmes were the basis for highly successful state initiatives in California, Massachusetts and elsewhere in the USA. According to the author, private-sector organisations should assume a leadership role in forming these collaborations, and take on several different roles and responsibilities, including: the provision of political support and encouragement for the production of scientific reports, policy papers and similar material that government agencies may find uncomfortable, try to delay or even attempt to scrap; and the holding of governmental agencies to account for using resources wisely and fulfilling their obligations to taxpayers. The latter occurred in California when administrators reduced the revenues of the existing tobacco control programme. The critics of this programme launched a highly successful media campaign, which helped to reduce tobacco consumption, improved the programme's effectiveness and returned it to full funding (Balbach and Glantz, 1998).

Other efforts in this area are focusing on using appropriate amounts of the funds from the Master Settlement Agreement (obtained from the settlement of lawsuits against the tobacco industry) for tobacco use prevention and control activities (Centers for Disease Control and Prevention, 1999), given that the majority of those revenues are being diverted to non-health uses by state legislatures. The coalitions funded by the Robert Wood Johnson Foundation Smokeless States National Tobacco Policy Initiative are prime examples of PPPs in this area. This initiative, administered by the American Medical Association, began in 1993 and has grown to become the third largest national initiative in tobacco control in the USA, exceeded in scope only by the federal government and the American Legacy Foundation. With coalitions in 42 states and the District of Columbia, 'Smoke-Less States' projects primarily address policy initiatives in three key areas: increasing the price of tobacco products; clean indoor air regulations; and increasing access to and reimbursement for tobacco use cessation. Typically, a state coalition is led by a voluntary health agency (e.g., the American Cancer Society), state medical society or a non-profit agency, and has representation from a wide variety of groups from the private health, business, education and youth sectors. These coalitions work actively with state and local health departments to promote comprehensive tobacco control plans and provide funding levels compatible with their success and governmental accountability.

Sparer (1999) discusses the changing nature of Medicaid in the USA, which he states has always involved a PPP. Medicaid provides health insurance to the poor, as opposed to Medicare, which provides health insurance to the aged and disabled. The original Medicaid programme mainly involved private, not-for-profit health care providers, and although it had its flaws, the author feels that it did a lot of good. Changes were introduced to the programme during the early 1990s, which attracted more commercially oriented health maintenance organisations (HMOs) into the partnership. The idea was that these commercial HMOs and provider-sponsored health plans would compete for Medicaid business, which would give its beneficiaries both more choice and better quality at a lower cost. However, despite the fact that these changes 'have shifted certain tasks previously performed by public entities to the private sector' (p. 153), the author does not feel that this has shifted the power to the private partner, as in fact the role of government has increased. Indeed, it now has several new administrative tasks, including 'setting capitation rates, helping clients choose between competing health plans, and establishing programs to protect the medical safety net' (p. 153).

PPPs in behavioural health care have been investigated by Egnew and Baler (1998). The authors proposed a potential arrangement whereby 'public behavioral health authorities retain their principal role as the single point of responsibility while collaborating with for-profit managed care organizations (MCOs) for specific administrative or technologically based services' (p. 571). This was seen as preferable to PPPs, where the respective roles of the public and private sector are seen as solely purchaser and provider. The role of the MCO would vary according to the specific needs of a public authority and the particular capabilities of the MCO, but could include such activities as training, consultation, technical assistance, the provision and maintenance of managed care, clinical quality oversight, financial modelling and projections, the maintenance of a provider network database and general administration. The role of the public sector would again vary, but would be seen mainly as one of managing all aspects of the system, operations and policy and may or may not include the provision of direct services. In effect this would allow the public sector to acquire the use of both sophisticated technology and skills without the need to incur capital outlay expense or maintain a number of managed care functions that would not be used all the time. It could therefore maintain overall control of a system, but call on the private sector's up-to-date expertise as and when it needed it.

Iida et al. (2005) considered PPPs as one of a number of vehicles that could be used to assist families which suffer from substance abuse and mental health problems. Their paper describes the *Starting Early Starting*

Smart (SESS) initiative, which involved collaboration between the Substance Abuse and Mental Health Services Administration of the US Department of Health and Human Services and Casey Family Programs (CFP), a private operating foundation. The initiative was developed and implemented in 12 geographically and culturally diverse cities during 1997–2001, and encouraged federal, state and local PPPs. The role of CFP was to provide funds to conduct certain research activities and disseminate SESS products, and also convene annual conferences for SESS stakeholders, policymakers and experts. Its 'staff contributed their knowledge and expertise in community-based collaboration, child welfare research and (the) development of community tool kits' (p. 218). Overall, the authors state the initiative was a success and that this was down to certain criteria, which those looking to launch similar projects could learn from. These were as follows: the importance of devoting adequate resources to the collaborative process; investment in face-to-face interaction and information sharing; a consensus approach to decision-making; the encouragement of divergent perspectives from stakeholders; the evolution of the collaboration from an emphasis on a single forum to electronic communications, work groups and an executive committee; and the teaming of public agencies and a private foundation.

A successful PPP in oral health, namely the Central Massachusetts Oral Health Initiative (CMOHI), has been described by Silk et al. (2010). However, despite its importance, the private-sector contribution to CMOHI may seem fairly minor compared to other projects. The aim of CMOHI was to promote oral health access to those who are not able to afford it, and its focus was Worcester City and parts of Worcester County in central Massachusetts. Worcester City has a population of 175,000, 17.9% of whom are below the federal poverty level. Private-sector involvement came via private practice dentists who were asked to both increase the number of Medicaid (referred to as MassHealth in Massachusetts) patients they deal with and donate time seeing poorer patients at a central location. This was then built on by recruiting these private dentists to become MassHealth providers. It could be argued that such an arrangement does not really constitute a PPP, and this will be further discussed in Chapter Nine.

EDUCATION

As Levin (1999) points out, businesses have a long tradition of establishing partnerships with schools and are motivated by both self-interest and altruism. In the USA, PPPs date back to the adopt-a-school programmes that originated in the 1960s with aims that included improving inner-city schools and providing employment opportunities to disadvantaged students (Burt and Lessinger, 1970). Notwithstanding, there has always been a certain amount of suspicion whenever the private sector gets involved with education, particularly with regard to primary and secondary schools.

Whilst there is no doubt that schools benefit from funding made available by companies such as IBM in the USA (see Boyles [2011] for other private companies involved in schools in the USA) and Tesco in the UK, there is always a feeling that such organisations are using this activity as a form of advertising for impressionable young minds. Another benefit, apart from funding, that private companies are seen to bring to schools is innovation, both in what the students learn and how they learn it, and when involved in the design of the school, as in the UK, better layouts and a more motivational environment (see, for example, Connolly and Wall, 2009, p. 112).

Some of the other criticisms regarding PPPs in the UK education sector are as follows. Rikowski (2003) views them as part of a process of the privatisation of teaching, with responsibility for many day-to-day issues moving from school governors and local education authorities (LEAs) to profit-seeking, private-sector companies (Whitfield, 2005), and schools being compelled to compete with one another for resources (Whitfield, 2006). Indeed, Hatcher (2006) suggests that the UK government no longer envisages LEAs as providers of education services but as brokers between schools and private suppliers of such services. Finally, West and Currie (2008, p. 201), based upon an analysis of private-sector involvement in UK schools, believe 'that the private sector in PFI contracts emerges as a powerful—if not the most powerful—stakeholder'. In the USA Boyles (2011) states that the involvement of commercial organisations in schools leads to an assumption that capitalism is the only or best economic theory and that, faced with commercial rewards, 'students see their role as seeking "right" answers to questions instead of searching for meaning by questioning, contesting, and antagonizing' (p. 445). Whilst PPPs that result in the building or refurbishment of a school tend not to happen in the USA, there have been projects of this nature. For example, in 1999 construction began on the Oyster School/Henry Adams House in Washington, DC (see Chapter Nine for an outline of how this PPP was financed). This resulted in the 'combination of a new public elementary school and a luxury apartment building on the site of an existing 73-year-old public school building' (Stainback, 2000, p. 129). Moreover, from 2010 onwards a number of PPPs have been used to install synthetic turf fields at US high schools (Hobbs, 2011).

Fitz and Beers (2002) compared the use of profit-making education management organisations (EMOs) in the USA and Great Britain (specifically England and Wales). It was noted that not only are EMOs in the USA a growing source of revenue for private companies, but also these organisations are moving into the UK (Palast, 2000) and Asian markets. Interestingly, Fitz and Beers (2000, p. 138) highlight the fact that 'the privatisation of education on an international scale has been encouraged by a little known agreement at the Uruguay meeting of the World Trade Organisation (WTO) that member states should promote the further "liberalisation" of public services, including education (Hirtt, 2000; WTO, 2002). In other words, the WTO agreement seeks an expanded role both for market forces and for private investment in education and member states are expected to develop appropriate policy frameworks'. In the UK, two educational initiatives where private funds were sought to create and maintain new kinds of public education were the City Technology Colleges (CTCs) and Education Action Zones (EAZs), neither of which was overly successful (see Whitty et al. [1993] and Mansell [2001] with regard to CTCs and EAZs respectively). Moreover, there have been a large number of UK schools built under DBFO contracts with mixed results. However, generally UK academics have been highly critical of such initiatives (see, for example, Ball et al., 2000, 2003b; Edwards and Shaoul, 2003; Hatcher, 2006; McCabe et al. 2001; McFadyean and Rowland, 2002).

According to Fitz and Beers (2002), educational governance in the USA is 'distributed across 50 states and some 15,000 school districts, each of which enjoys a considerable degree of autonomy' (p. 146). This means that each school district is free to privatise elements of its operation, including the management of its schools. One example of this is the introduction of charter schools, which offer the prospect of new start-ups in the public education system and can be initiated by profit-making enterprises or charitable organisations. Another distinguishing feature of PPPs in the USA is the number and size of EMOs, which are 'ready to invest in public sector take-overs and/or supply educational services' (p. 146). Private-sector participation in education includes organisations providing educational services and financial institutions that provide the funds for such businesses to take over schools. Therefore, there are well-established channels for organisations to invest in take-overs of public education, with investors clearly seeing an opportunity to obtain a return on their money. Compared to the UK, the scale of this sector is vast and it has a sophisticated infrastructure to sustain its continued growth. It should be pointed out that not all EMOs are profit-seeking, but those that are would operate either a single school or a number of schools. This latter option clearly results in efficiency savings as a private contractor bids to manage clusters of schools rather than bidding for each one separately. This is similar to the now defunct BSF scheme in the UK (see Chapter Two), where a single bid was made to DBFO a number of schools in a geographic area. One of the measures used by EMOs to denote success is a reduction in the costs associated with the delivery of education; however, it has been argued that they reduce such expenditure by either employing less experienced teachers or using uncertified staff (Furtwengler, 1998a, 1998b).

Two organisations that have tried to manage a number of schools in order to make a profit are Edison Schools, Inc. and Tesseract Group, formerly known as Educational Alternatives Inc.; however, according to Fitz and Beers (2002) neither has 'been as successful as either the corporations or privatisation advocates predicted' (p. 150). The authors suggest the following factors have contributed to this less than satisfactory outcome: no clear evidence of increases in student test scores has been found once changes in the social composition of schools have been accounted for; the anticipated efficiency savings have not occurred; teachers' organisations and community groups opposed to privatisation have mounted well-organised and well-publicised critical evaluations of privatisation initiatives (e.g., American Federation of Teachers, 2001); and the relatively low levels of per capita funding for public schools have made it difficult to make a profit without offering parents additional services. However, despite these setbacks there are two features in the USA which have led to the continuation of privatisation in this sector: the creation of a capital market targeted at public education; and the cumulative roll-out of charter schools. The tier of venture capitalists and the resources they can now draw upon enables service providers to pursue take-overs and charter school development without resorting to the DFBO type of PPP that is common in the UK education sector.

Longoria (1999) investigated smaller scale interventions of the private sector in education, categorising them at three levels. A level 1 programme is limited in scope and includes student incentive programmes whereby good performance is rewarded by coupons that can be exchanged for items such as confectionary and clothing from local, private sponsoring organisations. Other level 1 partnership activity includes the donation of used equipment to schools and the provision of free curriculum materials that, in many cases, are little more than veiled advertisements or designed to communicate a pro-business perspective (Molnar, 1996). Indeed, with some of the aforementioned incentive programmes, the line between public relations and advertising campaigns is blurred. Level 2 includes mentoring and scholarship programmes, and, compared to level 1 programmes, these are usually ongoing rather than one-time special projects and have more ambitious goals. However, they 'rely on the initiative of volunteers and sponsors for the content of activity rather than formally coordinated and established commitments' (Longoria, 1999, p. 319). Level 3 programmes also include ongoing partnership efforts, such as company-sponsored employee voluntarism, financial assistance in support of after-school programmes, and participation in shared decision making or other advisory committees that support the instructional goals of the school (Houston Independent School District, 1995). At this level the programmes are more formal in terms of institutionalisation and more comprehensive in scope than the other two and include involvement from national non-profit 'foundations such as the Ford, Joyce foundations, private businesses, and state and local agencies' (Longoria, 1999, p. 319). These non-profit foundations also get involved in fundraising activities for the schools. Whilst broadly supportive of such PPPs, Longoria (1999) concludes by stating that businesses needed to become more effective at targeting schools based on need, or equity could become an issue.

Dumort (2000) looked at the use of PPPs when it came to extending the use of internet-based off-campus courses in higher education in order to respond to changing trends. He states that one of the critical success factors for universities 'lies in their ability to address the lifelong learning market in collaboration amongst themselves but also with private partners' (p. 554). In order for new media to enrich educational choices on a sustainable and cost-effective basis, new business-academic partnership models need to be developed. He goes on to state such models would involve partnerships between software and telecommunication companies, broadcasters and publishers, for-profit educational organisations (more common in the USA) and academic providers. As a result educational services would be enhanced by exploiting the core competencies of all actors concerned; for example, the private-sector suppliers 'would provide the internet and communication infrastructures, and the academic institutions would keep responsibility and control over course content, the selection of students and their certification' (p. 554). It could be argued that such an arrangement does not really constitute a PPP, as the suppliers are merely providing a service, albeit in a collaborative manner (see Chapter Nine). However, as in the UK, PPPs are used in the USA to build student housing and other facilities at universities (see Mc-William [1997] and Stainback [2000] for respective UK and US examples).

A different level of education was investigated by Patterson (2004), who conducted a study of one state's Early Childhood Initiative partnership between local non-profit childhood centres and private firms. Her findings indicate a decrease in centre directors' focus on their education programmes and a reduction in parent participation. Many of the 46 centre directors interviewed for the study said that the advent of the PPP initiative found them spending more time soliciting donations from their corporate partners and parents reducing their participation in centre governance and policy due to a perception of marginalisation. 'Moreover, instead of identifying what parents of young children needed, the early childhood partnerships' focus shifted to what businesses needed for their current and future workers' (p. 166). This led to the common problem of an uneven partnership, with the influence of less powerful parents, community groups and even service providers being no match for the substantial influence of business. However, there were also clear benefits from the partnership; the board members from the private companies were thought by other members to add value through their critical thinking skills, orientation to innovation and a strong valuation of efficiency that improved management and decision making at the centres. Furthermore, the influence of the corporate sector resulted in expanded services to young children and their families and raised awareness of the needs of an often neglected sector of society.

CONCLUSIONS

In the USA the private partners in PPP contracts in both health and education rarely get involved in the building of either schools or hospitals, and therefore a lot of the criticisms that have been levelled at the initiative in the UK do not apply. Furthermore, the private sector has a long history of involvement in the US health sector, and whilst all health-related PPPs are not free from controversy or without their faults, they are in many ways a continuation of normal practice. However, education still remains a fairly contentious issue due to the private sector becoming more involved in the running of schools in the USA. Whilst the research has underlined some of the benefits the private sector can bring to schools (e.g., better access to funding, critical thinking, innovation, a greater focus on efficiency), a number of disadvantages have also been outlined. The first is the common perception of advertising or public relations masquerading as assistance when businesses give vouchers to star pupils or purchase much-needed equipment for schools. There is also the suggestion that private-sector involvement does not lead to any increase in the overall performance of the school; however, this might be partly due to resistance from teaching organisations and local communities. Equity has also been the subject of some concern, with businesses being accused of going for the better-performing schools and not targeting schools on a needs basis. A final disadvantage is that of marginalisation, whereby some parents and community groups feel they are no match for private companies and thus cease to assist with the running of the school. It was also noteworthy that there are well-established channels for accessing capital available to organisations looking to get involved with managing a school in the USA.

6 Public-Private Partnerships in the USA, Part IV
Other Sectors

This chapter looks at some of the other areas where PPPs have been used in the USA. It begins by looking at how the scheme has been used to enhance R&D and other business initiatives, before moving on to another highly contentious area, that of prisons. It then considers the use of PPPs in defence, waste management and water-related projects before looking briefly at other areas such as nuclear power and space exploration. It concludes by looking at research in two areas that have been widely covered in the UK literature, contract management and accounting and finance issues. However, due to the differing nature of the way that PPPs are financed in the USA, the latter has not been as widely addressed by academics from that country.

RESEARCH AND DEVELOPMENT

As Stiglitz and Wallsten (1999) highlight, governments have always played a role in R&D as it is crucial for a country's economic growth. In general they state that in the USA, industry funds the majority of product-related research, whereas government finances most fundamental or basic research. This public investment can be seen as filling in the gap left by the private sector's reluctance to invest in activity that may not provide sufficient returns; however, such underinvestment is not good for society as a whole and therefore governments step in.

Link and Scott (2001) state that PPPs have a role to play in improving technology R&D, their objective being to mitigate the problems of appropriating sufficient returns and risk that could occur in a dynamic market with substantial competitive pressures. The authors discuss the Advanced Technology Program (ATP), through which the US government shares research costs with industry (for a further discussion of this and other government programmes that support R&D see Stiglitz and Wallsten, 1999). Jaffe (1998) argues that for ATP to be effective it should select only those projects that would not be funded by the private sector in the absence of ATP funding, or if funded would be funded at a considerably lower level so that only partial results would have been realised and these results would have taken longer to occur. Link and Scott (2001) conclude that ATP project funding reduced the risk to the private firm and gave a socially worthwhile rate of return. They also state that in order for PPPs of this nature to be effective three premises were required. The first is that the private sector knows more than the government about the investment characteristics of the technology projects. Second, the government desires to overcome the project's underinvestment resulting from market failure at the least cost to the public. Third, all parties related to the PPP want to overcome the potential for opportunistic behaviour by the other party—that is, they should be incentivised to participate in the project in a way that maximises the total value of the project's expected outcome rather than the value to the individual partner.

In an earlier paper on technology R&D, Link (1999) outlines three broad objectives for PPPs: to leverage the social benefits associated with federal R&D activity; to enhance the competitive position of industry in the global marketplace; and to leverage industrial R&D to meet military or defence needs. He goes on to list six areas, including the aforementioned ATP, where he feels PPPs have been effective. In 1996 the Office of Technology Policy produced a report in which it was clearly supportive of technology partnership programmes and also produced a number of recommendations as to how they should operate. Link (1999) is fairly guarded about this report and feels two questions needed be asked. Firstly, is there a clearly defined market failure motivating the establishment of the PPP? Secondly, if it can be established that there is a market failure, then is direct funding through a PPP the appropriate policy response mechanism?

In a later piece of related work Link et al. (2002) review what they call strategic research partnerships (SRPs), which involve 'firms, universities, non-profit organizations, federal research laboratories, and public agencies' (p. 1459). SRP appears to be an umbrella term for the arrangements outlined in the earlier work on technology R&D, although it also embraces private-private partnerships. In order to be categorised as a PPP, the SRP has to receive some level of support from a public body, including direct subsidies, shared use of expertise and laboratory facilities and tacit licensing agreements. There has been a growing amount of investigation in the USA with regard to SRPs, although it is a fairly niche area compared to other PPP research.

Another area where PPPs could be employed to help with R&D is that of international agricultural research (Spielman and von Grebmer, 2006). The authors' focus is research that could improve the lives of poor people in developing countries and therefore is not of direct relevance to the USA. However, several institutions and organisations from that country have been involved in research that benefits poorer nations. For example, the Consultative Group on International Agricultural Research (CGIAR) is located in Washington, DC, and this has formed PPPs with a number of leading multinational organisations involved in agricultural research, including Monsanto and Dow AgroSciences, both US companies. Moreover, a number of US organisations are involved in PPPs with some of CGIAR's research centres—namely, Pioneer Hi-Bred, the Rockefeller Foundation, Bayer Crop-Science, the Institute for Genomic Research and the Agricultural Research Service of the US Department of Agriculture. The authors feel that PPPs offer an effective means of addressing large and complex research problems in developing countries, providing a number of constraints can be overcome. The main constraints are seen to be 'persistent, negative perceptions across sectors' and the 'competition and risk associated with intellectual assets and financial resources. Secondary constraints included the fundamentally differing incentives facing each sector, and the costs. . . . associated with building and sustaining partnerships' (p. 299). However, they do feel that many of these constraints could be overcome through a variety of policy mechanisms and organisational strategies, including a more creative structuring of partnership arrangements, effective project management and increased dialogue between the partners.

OTHER BUSINESS INITIATIVES

Kamieniecki et al. (1999) investigated the use of a market-based approach to dealing with the problem of air pollution. Their paper looks at the move from direct government regulatory control of air pollution to a more private form of air quality management, namely the Los Angeles Regional Clean Air Incentives Market (RECLAIM) emissions trading system. Under this PPP, the government sets the parameters for the market-based system, 'establishes national standards and determines annual benchmarks for standards; however, the mechanism for controlling air pollution, along with the economic incentives, now rests in the hands of the market and the private sector' (p. 109). The authors wanted to test whether initiatives like RECLAIM were effective, efficient, equitable and democratic. Over its first three years, emissions under RECLAIM were far below the predicted equivalents for a purely government-led approach and therefore the initiative was seen as being effective in reducing certain air pollutants. It was also felt that the RECLAIM initiative fulfilled the three necessary conditions for an efficient, competitive market in emissions credits: an adequate number of participants in the market; low transaction costs; and sufficient monitoring and enforcement by government.

Equity is concerned with whether all citizens benefit from an initiative. Under the trading system, those who reduce their emissions 'by more than the required amount can sell pollution credits to other firms that exceed their limits' (Kamieniecki et al., 1999, p. 108). There is always a fear that such a system gives certain companies a licence to pollute (Stavins, 1998); even though RECLAIM did lead to lower emissions overall, certain sectors of the population were denied the benefit of having the same level of cleaner air. Therefore the initiative was not seen to be completely equitable (Kamieniecki et al., 1999). The main concern regarding democracy is whether market-based approaches seriously restrict public input in the policy process, as decisions on the means of achieving a reduction in emissions are placed solely in the hands of private companies. Conversely, it could be argued that such an arrangement 'creates new possibilities for democratic participation through the purchase and trading of emissions credits' (p. 119). The authors are less clear as to whether RECLAIM was democratic; on the one hand the initiative has been criticised due to a lack of public access to market information, yet on the other hand public input and oversight were taking place 'in the form of working groups, advisory committees, and steering committees' (p. 119). Overall, the authors feel such constructive partnerships were an improvement on the traditional adversarial relationships between various stakeholders; however, they stress the vital role that a governmental agency has to play with regard to standard setting, compliance and the co-ordination of trading. Likewise, the concerns regarding both equity and public involvement would need to be addressed.

Another business area that PPPs could enhance, according to Kasarda and Rondinelli (1998), is that of manufacturing agility, which is seen as essential in an era of global competition. They state that there are two approaches in the USA to address the infrastructure support needs of agile manufacturing, these being reactive and strategic. A reactive approach involves little co-ordination between the various stakeholders, and this would generally be the way that the support infrastructure for agile manufacturing was then being developed in the USA. The authors therefore feel the USA is behind Japan and Europe in this regard. The strategic approach identifies, develops and integrates all the infrastructural elements that will be needed by agile manufacturers as well as the sites where they can be supported. The example given of a PPP that has adopted this approach is the Global-TransPark (GTP) in North Carolina. At the time the article was written, GTP was very much in the development stage, but the authors state that the PPP would 'develop and manage 15,300 contiguous acres . . . as a synergistic industrial transportation center and link it to other countries to provide a supporting environment for firms competing in international markets' (p. 76). They identify four elements of the external infrastructure that could create considerable competitive advantage: multimodal transportation systems; integrated telecommunications networks; commercial and service support; and knowledge centres. Since this article was written there has been a mixed reaction to GTP. Local people see it as a huge waste of their taxes (Anon, 2008); however, it has created jobs within the area and has a number of high-profile tenants (North Carolina GlobalTransPark, 2011).

PPPs are also seen a useful way of bringing together key stakeholders in the insurance of catastrophic events such as hurricanes and technological disasters (e.g., the explosion of Union Carbide's chemical tank at Bhopal, India) (Kunreuther, 2000). The sheer cost of paying out against natural, technological and environmental hazards is putting insurance and reinsurance companies in danger of insolvency or significant losses that will threaten the availability of future coverage (Kunreuther and Roth, 1998). Kunreuther (2000) sees three PPP programmes that could be set up in order to reduce losses from future disasters. The first of these is building codes, whereby properties are constructed in a way that protects them as far as possible from potential disasters. Under such arrangements a variety of stakeholders would be involved, including: banks and financial institutions, which would both provide a seal of approval to each structure that meets or exceeds building code standards and possibly provide incentives such as lower mortgage rates; the building industry; qualified government inspectors to provide accurate information about whether existing codes and standards are being met; and insurers, which may wish to limit coverage to those structures that are given a certificate of disaster resistance. The second programme is premium reductions linked with long-term loans for mitigation measures that householders would undertake to minimise losses. The government would gain through such an arrangement as it is they who normally provide assistance for poorer families following a disaster, and these are the families seen as most benefitting from the programme. Finally he suggests that insurers should offer a lower deductible (e.g., the specified amount a loss must exceed before a claim is payable) for those investing in mitigation measures. Again, the government would gain by not having to pay out so much in assistance to affected families.

Rom (1999) looks at the role that private firms (both not-for-profit and for-profit) could play in the provision of welfare services in the USA. Such organisations are seen as more active in finding work for the unemployed, as opposed to simply handing out welfare cheques, which was traditionally associated with public-sector organisations. Therefore, private firms are seen as better equipped to promote self-sufficiency and have the ways and means to get jobs for their welfare clients. Moreover, private organisations are less hampered by rules and personnel policies and can thus respond more quickly to the different needs of their clients. Finally, it could be argued that private firms are more incentivised to perform more effectively, and at a lower cost, or the contract might not be renewed. Finding employment is obviously only one form of welfare, and the author looks at other areas where PPPs have been utilised, such as Medicare and Medicaid (see Chapter Five), food stamps, child support enforcement, child welfare and training (closely related to finding employment). His paper also looks at how PPPs have been used in the provision of welfare services in Wisconsin and Texas. He sees the chief issues for governments in developing PPPs for welfare services as: treating clients fairly; creating competition; crafting contracts carefully so that contractors are properly held to account; and monitoring performance. At the time the article was written it was felt that it was too early to say whether PPPs were delivering better welfare services and the research findings were mixed (US GAO, 1997). However, the author does feel that whilst private firms may not prove to be better than public ones, multiple, competitive entities may provide better welfare services than state monopolies.

PRISONS

Involving the private sector in the running of prisons raises a number of moral issues, despite any economic or efficiency gains that may be made. Minow (2003) states that punishment is fundamentally an activity of government and therefore it should not be contracted out to private providers. Moreover, as private operators charge the governments a daily-based rate for each inmate under their supervision (Bayer and Pozen 2005), their financial performance is dependent on the number of 'man-days' they can clock up. Therefore, the incentives to keep prisons at full occupancy rates are strong. Nonetheless, in the 1980s several states in the USA, including Texas, Louisiana and Tennessee, found a way to cope with the increase in the inmate population and the corresponding costs of operation and maintenance via the private sector. Although the decision to privatise prisons in the USA is frequently related with more conservative political cultures, there is evidence that even more liberal states adopted private management in response to budgetary constraints and prison overcrowding (Price and Riccucci, 2005). Cabral (2007) reports that there are approximately 270 privately operated correctional facilities in the USA, and by 2011 more than 30 states had adopted private solutions. According to the US Department of Justice (2009), by the end of 2008 these prisons were housing almost 128,524 inmates, which at the time was 8.5% of the inmate population of the state and federal correctional systems. In some states, such as New Mexico, around 46% of inmates are held at private facilities. Schneider (1999) points out that there are three possible PPP arrangements with prisons: private ownership of the prison facility; private use of and profit retention from prison labour; and private management of the facility. However, she states that the first and third of these arrangements are the most common.

Some research on private prisons in the USA has concluded that they are more effective in terms of cost-reduction (Archeoembeault and Deis, 1996; Guppy, 2003; Mitchell, 2003; Bayer and Pozen, 2005). However, public prisons appear to be more efficient in preventing escapes and providing a broader range of treatment, recreation, social services and other services to inmates. Indeed, Morris (2007, p. 333) found that private companies have 'suffered a shortage of qualified personnel at times', which could affect the quality of confinement. Furthermore, according to the same author, in the case of inmates with expensive medical conditions it is more cost-effective to bring them into state custody, which also strengthens the argument that quality can be sacrificed due to cost-cutting. Bayer and Pozen (2005) also looked into this area of lower cost leading to lower quality when they studied both public and private prisons in Florida. They found that the private, for-profit prisons were good at reducing costs, but the inmates were more likely to commit further crime on leaving prison than were those leaving public prisons. Their work therefore corroborates the findings of an earlier study of Hart et al. (1997). Thus, the short-term savings offered by for-profit over non-profit management are negated in the long run due to increased recidivism rates. However, Lanza-Kaduce et al. (1999) found lower recidivism rates in private prisons, which they attributed to a higher completion of rehabilitation programmes. Given the many legal, ethical and political complications associated with profit-seeking correctional facilities, Bayer and Pozen (2005) conclude that there should be a move away from for-profit facilities in Florida's juvenile justice system. In a similar study, Camp and Daggett (2005) perform a public versus private comparison in prisons managed by the Federal Bureau of Prisons to evaluate inmates' misconduct. Their findings show that private prisons do not perform as well as public prisons in this area.

Another, more extensive study, by Lukemeyer and McCorkle (2006), which looks at 873 correctional facilities in the USA (762 state facilities, 93 federal prisons and 18 privately operated facilities), observes that even though, as a group, private prisons were less likely to experience violence, private prisons with violence exhibited it at the highest rate. This suggests that among private prisons in the USA there may be two groups: one group that is very effective in controlling violence and one that is much less effective. However, it should be noted that the number of private prisons in their sample was fairly small. Therefore, it can be concluded that, given the incentive structure and the types of contractual arrangements between private operators and public authorities, there appears to be a trade-off between cost reduction and quality deterioration in the private provision of prison services in the USA. This finding has some resonance with a review of nine PPP prisons in the UK (NAO, 2003b), which concludes that they tend to be more cost-efficient and better than public prisons in areas relating to decency and purposeful activities for prisoners but marginally weaker in areas such as safety and security. Nisar (2007) also reports that out of seven UK PPP prisons that opened between 1997 and 2001, only one did not incur financial deductions for poor performance.

Seeing as most state governments require that private firms offer the service at 5–10% below what it would have cost the state (Schneider, 1999; Morris, 2007), it is no surprise that they are more cost-effective. However, Boardman et al. (2005) look at a PPP arrangement for the building of a correctional facility in Massachusetts, concluding that the project was both wasteful and risky. This was due to the use of a lease purchasing arrangement, which was 7.4% more expensive than conventional financing, and inflated sales pitches that camouflaged real costs and risks to the public. Despite certain reservations some writers believe that prisons are one area where the PPP initiative is advantageous (for example, Vining et al., 2005).

DEFENCE

PPPs in the area of defence have also been looked into in the USA. A study by the Rand Corporation (1999) on the value of PPPs for the Army showed that the military gained extensive benefits from joint efforts between the government and private industry, including the following:

- The ability to leverage assets, reduce capital investments, reduce costs or decrease outlays to achieve infrastructure, intellectual property or financial goals;
- An increase in the value of property and other assets; and
- The creation of new capacities or assets to help the Army accomplish the military mission.

An example of a defence PPP in the USA can be seen at Lackland Air Force Base in Texas, where Landmark Organization Inc., a private firm, used its funds to build a new housing facility for enlisted personnel on land belonging to the Department of Defence (DoD). Landmark Organization's housing facility was provided more quickly and at a lower cost compared to that usually incurred by the DoD, saving taxpayers about $12 million over the life of the Lackland housing project (Ewoh & Dillard, 2003; NCPPP, 2004). However, Kee and Newcomer (2008) highlighted problems with a PPP between the US Coast Guard and a consortium of private defence contractors. The programme officer had developed a robust system of metrics to measure programme success by using a balanced scorecard approach, which was designed to help the partnership focus on key measures. However, because these measures were not developed prior to the formation of the partnership, the Coast Guard leaders felt they were playing catch-up and the measures were not fully supported by their private-sector partners.

Hibbert (2000) made the point that the UK's Ministry of Defence (MoD) tenders large amounts of work out to the private sector as 'the provision of goods and services is the core business of the private sector because it can frequently offer better value for money solutions for MoD capabilities. This allows the MoD to concentrate its efforts on its primary objective of delivering an effective front line service' (p. 40). UK defence projects are numerous and have included housing for Royal Air Force personnel at Cosford and Shawbury, roll-on roll-off ferries for rapid reaction forces, the refurbishment of MoD's main building at Whitehall, a new building at the Government Communications Headquarters in Cheltenham, an Army Foundation College in Harrogate, heavy equipment transporters and a training facility for Apache attack helicopters.

WASTE MANAGEMENT AND WATER

A report by International Financial Services London (2009) states that between 1997 and 2008 £2,635 million worth of waste management and water PPP projects were signed in the UK. However, such an amount represented only 4% of all projects signed off in this period. It can be seen therefore that this is not a major area of PPP activity in the UK when compared with sectors such as transport, health and education. Examples of such PPPs in the UK are the Alpha and Omega water projects in Northern Ireland and the Greater Manchester Waste Disposal Authority waste disposal and recycling project. Likewise there has not been a great deal of research in the USA in this area. Notwithstanding, the City of Indianapolis, Indiana, turned the maintenance and management of its wastewater treatment facilities over to a private vendor, resulting in nearly 50% savings reduction, from $30 million to $17 million in one year, whilst extending services to new areas. The $1.5 billion private water contract approved by the city council in March 2002 became the largest privatisation venture in the USA at the time (Clarke, 2003; NCPPP, 2002). A more problematic PPP was that of the Tampa Bay Seawater Desalination Plant, which was projected to process 10% of the water that the region's supplier, Tampa Bay Water, provided to the surrounding cities and counties (Vining et al., 2005). The desalination process was still an emerging technology at the time, and, although it was more expensive than conventional methods, pressure was being put on local authorities to reduce groundwater pumping. According to Vining et al. (2005) despite the chosen contractor, Covanta Tampa Construction, charging less for the water than expected, the relationship between them and Tampa Bay Water 'appears to have been fraught with mistrust, partly brought about by constant delays in completing the plant' (p. 207). Eventually the partnership was terminated, and, as well as having to pay the contractor $4.4 million for completed work, Tampa Bay Water ended up paying more per gallon of water and having to find other contractors to repair the filters and deal with other problems. As a local newspaper concluded at the time, the 'dumbfounding part of the troubled odyssey in opening this important desalination plant is that the contract arrangement was designed to limit the public's financial liability' (Anon, 2003, p. 14A).

A more successful water-related PPP, according to Shields (2011), is the water reuse system installed at the New England Patriots' Gillette Stadium in Foxborough, Massachusetts. This was brought in due to the considerable strain put on the local water supply and wastewater disposal systems when the New England Patriots are playing at home and the 'town's ranks temporarily swell more than fourfold' (p. 56). On such days 250,000 extra gallons of water are required and also need to be disposed of. Water is deemed to be reusable if it is not being used for drinking; therefore reused water can be used for activities such as flushing a lavatory, watering lawns and washing cars or laundry. The PPP consisted of the Kraft Group (the owners of the New England Patriots' football franchise), Applied Water Management (a subsidiary of American Water, the nation's largest investor-owned water and wastewater utility) and Foxborough itself, which issued public finance bonds. The model used was DBO and consisted of a decentralised water reuse system that also supported the natural water cycle by replenishing, or recharging, the area's groundwater (Shields, 2011). This PPP was deemed to be successful because it was 'self-sustaining, required minimal financial contribution from the town, protected the local environment, and promised mutual economic benefits' (p. 62).

Renckens (2008) considers how successful voluntary (i.e., no need for state regulation) PPPs have been with regard to electronic waste (e-waste) programmes. E-waste refers to the disposal of electronic products, which is a normal waste problem that is exacerbated by a high rate of obsolescence (e.g., computers and mobile phones) and the potential toxicity if such products are not disposed of properly. An earlier initiative known as the National Electronics Product Stewardship Initiative (NEPSI) held a series of meetings between 2001 and 2004 which included 'representatives from government (federal and state environmental agencies), industry (producers and recyclers) . . . and other stakeholders (research institutes and NGOs)' (p. 290). NEPSI eventually failed, although it did pave the way for future PPPs. For example, in 2003 the Plug-In To eCycling programme was launched, which was a PPP between the Environmental Protection Agency (EPA), local and state governments, consumer electronics manufacturers, retailers and service providers. However, as with NEPSI there were differences of opinion between the various partners and it was difficult to get some of the major private-sector stakeholders to participate. Notwithstanding, the programme has had some successes, with total recycling rates being somewhat higher following its launch. However, the take-back and recycling results of the Plug-In programme represented only a small fraction of the total amount of e-waste generated annually. Subsequently the EPA has attempted to bring together a multi-stakeholder group involving manufacturers, recyclers, NGOs, trade associations, refurbishers and states in order to establish a set of what are referred to as 'Responsible Recycler' practices. Generally the author believes that results to date have been limited and legislation seems inevitable, particularly as not all major companies participate in these PPPs or the resulting initiatives.

MISCELLANEOUS

The controversial area of nuclear power and how PPPs may have a role to play in its future development has been discussed by Rosenbaum (1999). Historically nuclear power in the USA was provided by a PPP arrangement involving government, its agencies and privately and publicly employed scientists and nuclear energy specialists. However, these early arrangements from the 1950s onwards were not only expensive for the taxpayer but also badly planned with regard to facility management, and there was also a lack of transparency and a failure to engage in 'a broad scientific and public debate on the technical and economic merits of nuclear power' (p. 77). Therefore, the development of nuclear reactors has stalled since the mid-1970s. The author gives a number of reasons why current energy arrangements will be insufficient to satisfy increasing future demands, including the greenhouse gases created by fossil fuels and the low percentage of energy provided by renewable sources (e.g., solar power). He makes a number of propositions for any future PPP arrangements, including: the need to be less secretive and actively involve 'environmental, public interest, and other citizen-based organizations' (p. 85); and better training for the managers of the future facilities, particularly when it comes to dealing with the political and social dimensions of the technology.

PPPs have also been seen as a means of accelerating the movement of mankind into space (Taylor et al., 2008). In a thought-provoking piece of research, the authors propose that PPPs could be used as a method of bringing governments and for-profit space organisations together in order to stimulate the private-sector financing necessary for commercial space development. They state the public sector would be responsible for the existing technology, government markets, hardware and the bureaucracy surrounding space travel, whereas the private partners would provide innovation, lower costs (through competition), commercial markets and investment. Indeed, because the US government ceased its space exploration programme in 2011, greater private-sector involvement seems inevitable.

Ghere (2001a) looks at PPPs from a slightly different angle when asking what private-sector firms had to lose by entering into partnerships with government organisations. The majority of PPP research would always assume that it is the private sector that has the most to gain from partnerships, as they stand to make a profit from providing a resource that is assumed to be the responsibility of the public sector. Thus there is an implicit feeling that should the PPP run into any problems that could lead to a service not being offered to the public, government will have to step in and bail out the contractor. Whilst entering into PPPs has not always meant profit for the private sector, there have been several instances in which the UK government has had to assist with problematic projects. For example, the taxpayer met a shortfall of £10.15 million following problems with the UK Passport Agency's computer system (NAO, 1999), and when the Royal Armouries Museum ran into difficulties in the summer of 1999, the government rescued it with a grant of around £1 million per year (Timmins, 1999). Indeed, Lovrich (1999) states that government is expected to fulfil the policy responsibilities of failed private-sector partners. One issue Ghere (2001a) investigated was that of intellectual property (IP), particularly in the area of patents. Again, the scenario used in this paper is different in that it envisages small private-sector companies looking for funding, rather than the large organisations normally associated with entering into contracts with the public sector. As well as any product associated with the contract, he asks whether IP could include performance-related expertise, system-generated efficiencies or even financial deal-making skills. He also considers whether the public sector brought any IP into a PPP agreement and whether attributes such as political skill in mobilising community support would fall within this category.

CONTRACT MANAGEMENT

Whilst there are clearly a whole range of issues that could come under this heading, one of the main items discussed in the academic literature is the competence of the public sector with regard'to complex contract negotiations and the subsequent monitoring of PPP projects in operation. There is a suspicion that UK public-sector employees are often at a disadvantage when dealing with contractors and their consultants, due to reservoirs of expertise not being built up in more commercial areas. It is therefore felt that building proper institutional capacity to create, manage and evaluate PPPs is a critical element in supporting the PPP process (OECD, 2008). This changing role of public-sector employees, and the fact that they are now expected to manage complex contracts, has been widely studied in the USA (see, for example, Romzek and Johnston, 2002; Brown and Potoski, 2003; Forrer and Kee, 2003; Bloomfield, 2006; Brown et al., 2006), with Lawther (2004, p. 129) making the point that 'effective PPPs require public officials to adopt unfamiliar roles'. Interestingly, Garvin (2010) believes that the USA could learn from the international community (including the UK) when it comes to increased public-sector staff capacity and a reducing reliance on external consultants. He states that 'deliberate actions such as establishment of best practices groups, development of principles and guidelines, and creation of standard procedures have all contributed to this growth' in other countries (p. 409). He states that advice is required in the following areas: establishing PPP policies and programmes; identifying candidate PPP projects; conducting business case analyses to determine the proper delivery strategy; defining project outputs and metrics; procurement processes and project delivery; and contract/partnership management. Ghere (2001b) also looks at the role of the public manager in PPP projects, stating that they need to rework 'a meaningful definition of local accountability that can provide clarity in integrating community expectations with the operational realities of privatization' (p. 315). Moreover, these expectations must include an anticipation that a number of problems are likely to arise over a long-term contract. Therefore programmes and processes need to be established to institutionalise private-sector provision around community values, an action that will benefit both the community and the private operator. He predicts that there may come a time when citizens come to the conclusion that certain services—for example, water and foster care—are no longer seen as a public issue, but merely a commodity to be purchased. See also Rosenau (1999, p. 25) for recommendations as to how PPPs are likely to more successful if certain guidelines are followed.

Ricaurte at al. (2008) also see the roles of civil engineers being extended due to the widening use of PPPs, as now they are now being exposed to knowledge areas such as finance, risk analysis, public policy and conflict resolution. The authors believe that civil engineers have a prominent role in the conception, evaluation and development of PPPs due to the fact that most schemes of this nature are utilised to develop civil infrastructure systems. Therefore, not only are these projects traditionally designed and constructed by civil engineers, but also such professionals can provide better assessment and life cycle perspectives for their development. Moreover, once the project is in the operational phase they can enhance its operation and maintenance due to their participation in the design process. Therefore, civil engineers would need more than just technical skills and would need to get involved in finance and managerial decision-making, as well as be able to act as independent monitors of performance-based PPPs. They conclude by stating that the current civil engineering curriculum would need to be reviewed and modified and that new graduate programmes that address delivery methods for infrastructure projects, such as PPPs, would need to be developed.

Boardman et al. (2005) highlight the difficulty of capturing transaction costs in any comparison between partnerships and traditional project delivery and catalogue 76 major North American PPP projects as part of this research. They note that less than half of these PPPs include a significant private financing role. Five transportation, water-supply and waste-disposal projects are presented, showcasing a series of 'imperfect' partnership projects with high complexity, high asset specificity, a lack of public-sector contract management skills, and a tendency for governments to be unwilling to 'pull the plug' on projects once under way; all of which conspired against the simple notion that partnerships guarantee either political or commercial success. The authors highlight the fact that private entities are adept at making sure, one way or another, that they are fully compensated for risk-taking and even strategic behaviour such as declaring bankruptcy (or threatening to go bankrupt) in order to avoid large losses. There is therefore a tension; on the one hand governments need to hold their nerve and watch commercial failures materialise as risks are borne by commercial entities, but on the other they yearn to be viewed as successfully governing a growing and vibrant market economy. As will be seen in Chapters Seven and Nine, the establishment of dedicated PPP units in the USA is beginning to take place, and this is due to the influence of a number of countries, including the UK.

ACCOUNTING AND FINANCE

The area of accounting for PPPs has been the subject of a great deal of debate in the UK. The perception that PPP was viewed as a means of keeping contracts 'off balance sheet' led to the publication of *Application Note (AN) F to Financial Reporting Standard 5, Reporting the Substance of Transactions* (Accounting Standards Board, 1998), to help clarify which party should record the asset (and related liability) on their balance sheet. However, AN F and the subsequent HMT (1999) guidelines did not end this debate due to the subjective nature of both sets of guidelines. This had the potential to lead to risk being incorrectly transferred to the private sector, primarily in order to remove the asset from the public sector's balance sheet (Connolly et al., 2008). However, despite these concerns, more PPP assets did appear on the public-sector balance sheet (see HMT, 2006), not that this prevented off-balance sheet debt being the subject of a House of Lords report in 2010. More recently the UK public sector has implemented international financial reporting standards. This has had a major impact on the accounting treatment of PPP assets, due to Interpretations Committee Interpretation (IFRIC) 12 (2006) stating that should any PPP arrangement be classed as a service concession then the related assets should appear on the balance sheet of the grantor of that succession (i.e., the public-sector purchaser). According to the Financial Reporting Advisory Board (2007), PPP-type contracts appear to exhibit the characteristics of service concession arrangements covered by IFRIC 12, and therefore the public sector should now include all PPP assets on its balance sheet. However, Heald and Georgiou (2011) state that the change of emphasis from risk and reward under AN F to control under IFRIC 12 could still lead to the manipulation of PPP schemes to keep them off the public-sector balance sheet.

Perhaps due to the fact that PPPs in the USA do not rely solely on private-sector financing (see Boardman et al., 2005), and they have never been about shifting expenditure off-balance sheet, the accounting for, and financing of, PPPs is not a particularly big research area. However, due to the severe economic problems the USA faced in 2011 and the fact that more private-sector funding was being called for, certain reports proposed transparent reporting should this occur (see, for example, Engel et al., 2011; and DiNapoli, 2011). In the UK the off-balance sheet debate with regard to PPPs has been an area of immense interest, and there have been a large number of articles on the subject (see, for example, Heald and Geaughan, 1997; Hodges and Mellett, 1999, 2004; Kirk and Wall, 2001, 2002; Heald, 2003). Work has also been done in other areas of finance in the USA. For example, Maskin and Tirole (2008) wrote a theoretical article that looks at spending limits and how, under certain agreements, private PPP contractors can circumvent these by accepting low initial payments in exchange for higher ones later on. This pushes the higher costs to another period in which another politician (local or otherwise) or political party may be in power. Another theoretical paper has been written by Pantelias and Zhang (2010), who propose a methodological framework for assessing the financial viability of PPP projects by evaluating their corresponding investment risk and apply this to a hypothetical transport project. Page et al. (2008) look at the role of private equity investment funds in PPP financing. They state that these funds do have a role to play, although a mismatch between their short investment duration and the length of some of the PPP contracts could present challenges, albeit ones that could be overcome. Moreover, as already stated, Bloomfield et al. (1998) state that a PPP lease-purchasing financing arrangement for a Massachusetts correctional facility was more expensive than conventional general obligation financing. See also the article by Gallay (2006) referred to in Chapter Three, which looks at PPPs that are used as a method of obtaining capital without seeking specific budget authority. Finally and as already suggested, it is perhaps noteworthy that Gapper (2008) states that the USA was looking enviously at the UK model of private finance to address infrastructure deficits. The financing of PPPs will be returned to in Chapters Eight and Nine.

CONCLUSIONS

This chapter has attempted to summarise other areas where PPPs have been used in the USA. As with urban regeneration, transport, health and education, success has been mixed, and, whilst PPPs have been seen to bring benefits in certain areas, they rarely appear to be an optimal solution. Governments will always have a role in the R&D of a nation as it is so vital to economic success; however, research has shown that certain conditions have to be met in order for PPPs in this area to be successful. As in other sectors, one of the key conditions is that no partner should seek to behave in an opportunistic manner, thereby jeopardising the maximum potential outcome of the project for all parties. With regard to other business initiatives, despite a number of successes there were sometimes problems with equity and the involvement of communities in PPPs. Despite these reservations it was seen that such arrangements had a part to play in dealing with air pollution, manufacturing agility, the insurance of catastrophic events and welfare services.

A more controversial area is private-sector involvement in the management of prisons. Overall, research has shown that whilst PPP prisons are often run at a lower cost than purely public ones, this has tended to lead to a fall in quality. Public prisons have a better record when it comes to the welfare of prisoners and also with regard to prisoners reoffending after being released. Little research has been conducted in the area of defence and, despite this being a sector where the mixing of private and public (in this case military) personnel might be expected to be fraught with difficulties, DoD PPPs appear to be fairly non-contentious. Opinions are more divided about two water projects and an e-waste initiative, with one water project being seen as more cost-effective than the other and voluntary PPPs in e-waste not being seen as sufficient to prevent legislation. Finally, there is some speculative research about the role PPPs could play in nuclear power and space exploration and an article looking at the IP that was created in partnerships. The chapter also considered the inexperience of public-sector officials at dealing with PPP contracts and their subsequent operation and accounting and finance issues, the latter being a far more divisive topic in the UK.

Before moving on to the chapters that deal with the empirical findings of this study, it is perhaps worth reflecting on what areas need further clarification. The literature reviewed in Chapters Three to Six presents a fairly mixed reaction to PPPs in the USA. It is argued that the criticism is not as pointed as it is in the UK, but it is apparent that there are still many problems that need to be overcome. It will be therefore interesting to establish the main objectives and drivers of PPPs in the USA and what lessons have been learnt from those that have not been successful. Although PPPs are clearly used for a wider variety of purposes than they are in the UK, the DBFO model is relatively rare, and it will be interesting to see if this is likely to change given the dire economic circumstances the USA is in at the time of writing. It will also be interesting to ascertain whether the USA has been influenced by any other countries as the PPP process continues to develop, and if the private-sector involvement in public service delivery is more accepted here than it is in parts of Europe. Finally, it will be worth noting if there are any differences in the factors considered beneficial or otherwise to the overall success of a PPP project. The next chapter presents the first part of the empirical findings, and that is the results of semi-structured interviews with key actors in the formulation and implementation of PPP policy in the USA and those who play more of an advisory role.

7   The Views of Key Stakeholders

METHODOLOGY

The empirical aspect of the research in this book utilises semi-structured interviews with key actors in the formulation and implementation of policy relating to PPP projects in the USA as well as those who play more of an advisory role. The reason for collecting qualitative data by informal, semi-structured interviews is based on the interactionist's premise that when the aim is to understand a complex process and where those involved have different perspectives on the matter in question, it makes sense to adopt a research strategy which allows these perspectives to be understood in the same terms in which the participants understand them (Blumer, 1969). This approach enables the researcher to 'access the perspective of the person being interviewed.... to find out from them things that we cannot directly observe' (Patton, 1990, p. 278). By conducting such interviews, research information can be gathered on issues such as drivers, benefits, problems and factors impacting upon the success of PPPs in the USA. It is hoped that this will help to explain why they have such a wider application in the USA (compared to the UK) and why the initiative appears to be far less controversial.

Representatives from 23 organisations were interviewed, although on three occasions two people from the same organisation participated in the interview, and therefore the views and responses of 26 interviewees are reported here or in subsequent chapters. The interviewees were chosen because of their seniority and assumed detailed knowledge and awareness of the issues surrounding the implementation of PPPs and the formulation of the related policy. The interviewees were asked for their views on a series of issues such as: the objectives and drivers of PPPs; lessons that could be learnt from existing projects; the influence of other countries; and factors important to project success. The questions included in the interview guide (see Appendix) emanated from the main themes identified in both the academic and government literature relating to PPPs as well as press articles (see Chapters Three to Six). Typically each interview lasted approximately one hour, with the interviews being recorded and transcribed when allowed.

Table 7.1   Interviewee Classification

Role	Classification
Academic (A): Specialising in the area of PPPs in the USA.	A1-5
Member of a business improvement district (BID): Involved in a number of PPP schemes in a large city. BIDs are used in a number of countries including the UK; see British BIDs (2011) for more information.	BID1-2
Consultant (C): Employed within accountancy or other firms (including think tanks) that advise on PPP contracts.	C1-4
Legal adviser (LA): Providing assistance to states on the legal aspects of PPPs.	LA1
Media analyst (MA): Working in a leading USA newspaper and commenting on PPPs.	MA1
Member of a non-government organisation (NGO): Involved in the negotiation of PPP contracts with private-sector providers.	NGO1
Operator (O): Private-sector contractor involved in the provision of PPP services.	O1
Policy advisor (PA): Advises states on policy areas.	PA1
Policy implementer (PI): Responsible for implementing PPP policy in a federal/state department.	PI1-3
Policymaker (PM): Responsible for formulating PPP policy in a federal/state department.	PM1-2
Project financier (PF): Provides advice on finance for infrastructure projects.	PF1
PPP advisor (PPPA): Promotes the overall use of PPPs in the USA.	PPPA1
Representative of service providers (RSP): Member of an association representing the service providers in PPPs.	RSP1
Member of a transit authority (TA): Involved in a number of PPP projects in a large city.	TA1-2

Where this was not permitted, the author took notes and then wrote up any findings immediately after the interview to ensure that all salient points were recalled. Given the potential sensitivities of the matters being discussed and the desire for the participants to be as candid as possible, interviewees were informed that the interviews would be reported in a manner in which specific statements could not be attributed to particular individuals. To reflect the different focus of the interviewees, they were classified according to Table 7.1.

Due to the size of the USA and the wide number of areas in which PPPs are used, it was not possible to cover all geographic areas or sectors. Therefore, the upcoming findings and the case studies in Chapter Eight are without doubt centred around the East Coast, if not mainly Washington. Moreover, the only sectors covered in any detail were transportation, health and urban regeneration. However, these three areas are those in which PPPs are used the most, as the literature review highlighted. Moreover, transportation PPPs in the USA have most in common with the DBFO model most commonly commented upon in the UK. Notwithstanding, some of the consultants, academics and general promoters of PPPs who were interviewed had more general viewpoints on the initiative. It should be noted that one of the interviewees worked in the defence sector, and whilst some of his or her comments are included several were removed or reduced, following the interviewee receiving a draft copy of this chapter, due to the sensitive nature of this area. However, some useful points remain.

MAIN FINDINGS

It should be noted that the upcoming quotes are not necessarily verbatim, although changes have been made only to either protect an identity or improve understanding for the reader. Abbreviations have sometimes been used within the quotes, although these were not always the terms the interviewees used. The outline follows that of the survey in the Appendix; however, not all of the questions were answered by the interviewees. Moreover, in some cases a response to one question covered the area of another (e.g., maintenance of PPP assets). Therefore there are fewer questions here than there are in the original survey. Finally, some of the information gleaned from the interviews formed the basis for the case studies in Chapter Eight and the concluding comments in Chapter Nine.

Experience of Interviewees

Interviewees were initially asked to outline their background and both past and current experience so that their views and opinions could be placed in context. Each interviewee had extensive experience in their area, with all working in the area of PPP for at least five years. Some of the interviewees had always worked with PPPs, and in several cases those who hadn't had come from backgrounds that were conducive to working in this area—for example, engineering, accounting, policy-making and legislation.

Main Objectives of PPPs

The majority of answers for both this question and the subsequent one seemed to be framed in the context of the problems that the USA was facing at the time: crumbling infrastructure, reduced budgets and high unemployment—for example:

They are all about leveraging more dollars from taxpayer's money. (PM1)

They are needed to rebuild our disintegrating infrastructure whilst saving taxpayer dollars. (PPPA1)

Look at the recent initiative in DC to link the unemployed with businesses who get tax breaks and wage subsidies for hiring them. It shows what PPPs can do to galvanise things when times are hard. (C3)

The initiative being referred to is One City, One Hire, which was launched in Washington in September 2011. The idea is to match those out of work with local companies that also receive funding to train these new workers. It follows the model of Hire One Atlanta, a programme initiated earlier in 2011 that matched 5,000 unemployed people in the city of Georgia with local companies in the first six weeks.

Some comments, however, are not related to the economic difficulties of the time:

They allow the public sector to do things they could not do with their current skill set. (NGO1)

To accomplish what the public sector can't do alone, but there is also a bit of public relations in it for the private partners as it is seen as the right thing to do. Moreover, they want a seat at the table and access to the decision-making. (RSP1)

Main Drivers behind PPPs

There is a serious funding gap in this country at the moment, and it isn't going to go away. If we are to get this economy moving again, we need PPPs. (O1)

Take my state's infrastructure, which includes over 5,000 structurally deficient state-owned bridges. We cannot fund their renovation or rebuilding under state budgets or get the necessary money from the federal government. PPPs present us with a potential solution. (PM2)

The private sector has the capital ready and is willing to put it into infrastructure projects. (C4)

There is money available from a variety of sources including foreign investment banks and pension funds from all over the world; it is just up to the states to give the go ahead for the projects. (PF1)

They give access to a large amount of funding, but I would also say that they are a necessity due to the health care system in the USA. (RSP1)

Other interviewees believe that putting work out to tender forces prices down:

Consumers win whenever there's competition, and PPPs create competition. Even unsolicited bids make states sit up and think about what could be done to bring in a bit more revenue. (C2)

An unsolicited bid is where a contractor will approach a state with a proposal to, say, extend or renovate a road. This is not the same as when a PPP is put out to tender, where the idea has originated from the state's politicians and key decision makers. Another interviewee believes the private sector is also a driving force:

> Whether it is an unsolicited or a general bid, private companies are driving PPPs as they want the business. (LA1)

The increasing complexity of projects was also seen as a driver behind PPPs:

> Private-sector partners are much more in tune with changes going on in their own industry, particularly technological changes. Plus they have more incentives to bring in labour saving devices such as automatic tolling. (A3)
>
> Complexity can also be applicable to the structure of the contract. For example, the Colorado Eagle project for three transit lines was a huge PPP with eight different sources of funding. (LA1)

More general comments were also made, some of which indicate dissatisfaction with government and the public sector:

> The main drivers are problem solving and innovative ways of doing things at a cheaper cost. (NGO1)
>
> The private sector operates more efficiently with none of the political patronage associated with public projects. For example, an official wants to get re-elected so he creates jobs operating turnpikes. The private sector would seek to automate any toll roads to improve the flow of traffic. (PA1)
>
> If the public sector worked like it should there would be no need for PPPs—but they cannot raise and spend money efficiently or run and control projects effectively. (A5)
>
> They solve problems in a more efficient and innovative way than they are currently being solved by the public sector. However, I am not sure many of the projects that are labelled as PPPs are really them at all. Take Solyndra, this has been classified as a PPP, but I don't think it is. (A1)

The Solyndra case referred to was highly controversial in the autumn of 2011. In 2009 the US government had lent the company $535 million to build a factory where solar panels would be manufactured. Solyndra subsequently filed for bankruptcy in September 2011. This approach, in which the government lends money directly to companies in the energy savings sector, differs to that of the UK, in which households can apply for government grants and then deal with individual companies on a one-to-one basis. Notwithstanding, whether this is a PPP is debatable. This point is returned to in Chapter Nine.

Key Considerations When Deciding Whether to Use a PPP or Another Method of Service Delivery

One of the most common responses, which was to be expected, was that PPPs are *a*, as opposed to *the*, solution to problems facing a number of sectors. They work better in some areas than others, but they are not a silver bullet and are certainly not free.

> It must be remembered that PPPs are not the answer to all of our state's transportation and infrastructure problems, but I believe they can at least start to address the problems we face. (PM2)
>
> They work well on roads, but less so in schools, which are more locally controlled, and energy projects, as the private sector already plays a major part in this sector. What's more both states and local authorities can issue tax-exempt bonds, which is a very cheap way to borrow money so they may not need private finance. Other, smaller states such as Idaho and South Dakota prefer a 'pay as you go' method. (LA1)
>
> Not every new highway project in the state will be a toll road or involve private capital. Where all-public financing makes sense, the state will do that. (PI3)
>
> The key consideration is who can deliver the service better, but also in our case who is willing to provide funding. (NGO1)
>
> If funding is an issue then it is stated that more money can be leveraged by the use of PPPs, but I would say that if capital markets are working efficiently then the private sector should be able to fund some of these projects themselves and it should not be up to governments to come up with the money. (A1)

This last comment refers to certain types of PPPs used in the USA, some of which will be looked at in more detail in Chapter Eight. These are where the private sector initially uses public money to fund economic development projects. One final comment was as follows:

> PPPs are used in three cases—there is no public finance available, the public sector is unable to execute the project or there is a philosophy within a particul.ar state (for example, Virginia) to use PPPs. (BID2)

How Much Autonomy Does a State Have When It Comes to Deciding Whether to Use a PPP?

The answers for this particular question were virtually all the same. The federal system that operates in the USA means that states normally have total autonomy when it comes to deciding whether to use a PPP. They are usually in charge of infrastructure development, so they are the most interested in alternative ways of project delivery. Moreover, PPPs are endorsed by the federal government. However, it is interesting to note that not all states have decided to go down this route. At the time of writing, 31 states had PPP enabling legislation (National Conference of State Legislatures (NCSL), 2011), although this can vary between states (see Istrate and Puentes, 2011). Moreover, this figure is likely to increase over time as more states turn to PPPs for solutions to infrastructure problems. For example, in March 2011, legislation which enabled the state of Pennsylvania to enter into transportation-specific PPPs was passed, and in May of the same year the governor of Georgia signed legislation which allowed the option for PPPs in the development of water supply and infrastructure. A comment from one of the interviewees sums up this situation:

> The laws vary so much from state to state that investors often refer to the USA as a patchwork of 50 separate countries. (MA1)

This can create problems with PPPs that cross several state boundaries. Another interviewee (C1) referred to a project currently in the pipeline, which is looking to transmit clean, low-cost wind energy from its source in Guymon, Oklahoma, to the Tennessee Valley Authority system near Memphis. This energy could then be used by ten large metropolitan areas in the USA. However, despite a ready market for such a project in terms of private finance, the PPP is facing problems in fitting into each of the affected states' regulatory framework for transmission sites. This is proving particularly problematic in those states which the transmission line will cross, but that will not benefit from the energy.

However, states still have to rely on the federal government for credit in certain cases:

> Although states do not have to seek federal approval for a PPP, they may need to borrow money from initiatives such as Transportation Infrastructure Financing and Innovation Act (TIFIA) loans. Moreover, the Office of Innovative Program Delivery provides funding for projects which cannot be funded by the gas tax. (LA1).

One interviewee (A4) now sees TIFIA loans as a double-edged sword as demand now easily outstrips supply. Thus whilst a lot of states now want them there is not enough money to go around. Therefore, big political decisions will have to be made by the federal government as to which states get the money. In such cases the government could stand accused of favouring some states over others for political gain, a phenomenon referred to as pork-barrel politics. The gas tax is discussed in more detail in Chapter Eight.

Interestingly, according to RSP1, there is slightly less autonomy for states in the health sector. Under the Medicaid system, states need to submit planning amendments to the federal government periodically in order to receive the requisite funding. A system known as Federal Medical Assistance

Percentages is used, whereby percentage rates are used to determine the matching funds allocated annually to certain medical and social service programmes in the USA. The higher the percentage, which is inversely related to affluence, the more the state receives in matching funds from the central government. Therefore, states need to keep the federal government up to date with their changing requirements. The federal government also provides support and guidance to the states on health issues.

Has the US Policy with Respect to PPPs Been Influenced by That of Other Countries?

Certain responses to this question correspond to some of the more recent literature in the USA, which seems to be looking to the UK for influence. Whilst this will be discussed later in the book, it is noteworthy that there appears to be little evidence that any consideration of the drawbacks of some of the models being proposed had been undertaken.

> Not really as I feel the USA has always been engaged in PPPs of some nature. However, some policy makers have looked at the PFI model in the UK. (NGO1)
>
> The USA is starting to look at models such as the UK's public-sector comparator (PSC), but there is an awareness of the differences between the two countries. (LA1)
>
> One way other countries, such as the UK, Australia and Canada, have influenced policy in the US is the setting up of dedicated PPP units, which set guidelines and provide technical assistance amongst other things. Some states have created their own units, although progress is slow. (C1)

Other interviewees indicated that the USA was also looking further afield:

> We have a transatlantic group that looks at urban redevelopment in both the USA and Europe; I think we both learn from one another. (C4)
>
> Health spending has soared in the USA in recent years and it is far higher than the OECD average. So we have looked at health provision in a number of countries, some of whom are using PPPs. However, to date these have just been case studies and no changes have been recommended. (RSP1)
>
> The USA lacks a proper investment bank that can be used for PPPs. Both Europe and Australia have these. (PI3)

The banks referred to here are the European Investment Bank and Macquarie Capital respectively, both of which have been involved in a large number of PPPs, with the latter investing heavily in the USA. In 2011, President Obama reiterated his call for a national infrastructure bank, to support private-sector investment in projects that would revitalise the US domestic infrastructure. However, some writers believe that the Export-Import Bank of the USA, which finances multibillion-dollar infrastructure projects overseas, could fulfil this role (Schweitzer et al., 2011). The interviewee C1 was not so sure about this and said that it would be easier to start an infrastructure bank from scratch rather than try to change the role of the Export-Import Bank. However, C1 agreed that such a bank was essential in order to start channelling money from pension funds, which were keen to invest in PPP projects (see Chapter Nine). Several states have already set up their own infrastructure banks, with C1 believing that California's Infrastructure and Economic Development Bank (referred to as the I-Bank) provides a compelling model. After its initial capitalisation of $181 million in 1999, this bank has funded itself on interest earnings, loan repayments and other fees, and has supported over $400 million in loans (Hazelroth, 2010). It has also worked with one of the largest US pension funds, the California Public Employees' Retirement System, in relation to financing PPPs.

With regard to US banks in general, another interviewee (PF1) believes they stopped investing in major projects following the collapse of Enron. They then moved into the housing market and ran into problems there as well. Generally, therefore, they have lost their nerve when it comes to infrastructure investment. A final comment was:

> Some of the concessions (in transportation) have not worked out well for either the public or private partner. I know that some states are looking at what Spain and South Korea do to see if they have better models. (PM1)

The concession type of PPP contract is discussed in more detail in Chapter Nine.

What Lessons Can Be Learnt from Existing PPP Projects in the USA?

There are no real general lessons that could be applied to PPPs overall, but some interesting comments were made:

> I think an important lesson was learnt from the California 91 (Express Lane) PPP. That contract was signed with a non-compete clause, which led to severe problems when the state tried to build competing facilities to ease traffic congestion. Although this was eventually sorted out it did lead to changes in the nature of non-compete clauses in contracts. For example, most contracts now allow limited competition, such as the construction of small access roads parallel to the toll road. (PM1)

Despite obvious problems with non-compete clauses, Geddes (2011) still feels they are necessary, albeit in a modified format, to attract investors to transportation projects. Should potential financiers feel that the state or other authority is free at any time to build a competing facility that could have a serious impact on a tolled road that they are either going to buy or build, then they would have serious reservations about the feasibility of the project providing a suitable return. Another interviewee made the following observation:

> Politics can sometimes get in the way of perfectly good projects. Take the PPP in Florida where central funding was turned down as the local politicians didn't want to be seen to be wasting federal money. Likewise, a perfectly feasible PPP did not go ahead in Pennsylvania due to politicians taking too long to come to a decision. (LA1)

The Florida project refers to a high-speed rail that was to be built in the state. A partnership, including the UK's Virgin Group, was formed and was due to receive $2 billion from the federal government, but this was rejected by local politicians and the PPP fell through. The PPP in Pennsylvania was where the state was offered a concession fee of $12.8 billion for a 75-year lease on the tolled Pennsylvania Turnpike. As with some other concession deals, most notably the Chicago Skyway, this payment would have given the state the ability to pay off existing debts and still have a considerable surplus for investment (Geddes, 2011). However, as stated earlier, the deal collapsed to due to political delays. Another interviewee (PA1) believes that in some cases the opposite problem to that experienced in Florida occurs, in that states wait too long to try to get federal funding for a project. In a time of economic recession there are real needs and construction costs would be cheaper as companies are looking for work. However, feasible projects are not going ahead as states are trying to get as much money from the federal government as possible. Other comments are as follows:

> The quality of care has definitely improved due to PPPs and a lot of this is down to the measures that have been introduced as a result of the partnership. The next area we have to concentrate on is cost reduction. This won't necessarily mean that quality will suffer as we can look at areas such as doing away with duplication and the introduction of e-records. (RSP1)
>
> Firstly, the surplus money from the Chicago Skyway should have been spent on transportation projects and not social infrastructure. Secondly, politicians have to learn that a PPP is not free; the money will still be paid out at some stage. (PI3)

The first part of this comment echoes a common concern that any money that comes from transportation, such as tolls or concession fees, must go back into that sector, whether it is into roads or other forms of transit. The Chicago

Skyway PPP is mentioned many times in this book. It was felt that local politicians spent the surplus money from the concession fee on schemes that improved their image, rather than much needed transportation projects. Another interviewee, A4, agreed with the second part of the foregoing comment, feeling that decisions to go ahead with PPPs had often been based in the past on politicians' flawed conception that they were funded by the private sector alone. A final comment deals with the changing nature of PPPs:

> Following President Obama's first stimulus package the focus was on shovel-ready projects. It is now time to move on from those and look at transformative investments. (C1)

A shovel-ready project is one that is ready, or almost ready, to begin (see Sofge [2009] for a fuller description). According to C1, transformative investments trigger a profound change in physical infrastructure and the built environment that enables and accelerates the transition to, at either the metropolitan, regional or national scale, a productive, sustainable and inclusive economy. Examples of projects that fit with this definition are transit-oriented development projects (see Chapter Nine), urban regeneration projects involving former DoD land and buildings and transmission lines that will deliver low-cost wind energy from its source to high-energy users (this project was discussed earlier in this chapter).

The interviewees were then asked how important a number of factors were to the overall success of PPP projects.

Projects Completed on Time

There was a general consensus that this was one of the major benefits of using PPPs.

> This is really important and is far quicker under a PPP arrangement. There is none of the usual delays caused by political haggling over major issues such as funding, and minor ones such as how many trees should be planted on the side of a toll road. This means the facility can get built quickly and the revenues can start rolling in. Everybody wins, the driver gets a better facility, the state gets its money, depending on the deal, and the contractor can start collecting the toll money. (C3)
>
> This is very important. The quicker the project is built the quicker the investors get a payback on the money they have put in. (LA1)
>
> There is no doubt that involving the private sector gets houses built or renovated faster and at a lower cost than with military construction. (PI1)

The latter refers to houses built for military personnel. Over the past year major projects have been announced for the building of over 3,000 housing units for four air force bases and 202 houses and associated amenities at Fort Bliss, which is located in the states of New Mexico and Texas. The projects involve the private-sector partner developing, managing, constructing and renovating homes and other ancillary facilities and amenities at the military bases; however, the financing comes from the DoD.

Value for Money for the Taxpayer

As seen in Chapter Two this is one of the major considerations when deciding to go for the PPP approach, and it remains a contentious issue in the UK. However, it was not seen as particularly important by any of the respondents. However, this may change:

> Although a cost-benefit analysis is carried out, states tend not to go for VFM assessments that are commonplace in the UK. However, people are starting to look at models such as the PSC so it could become more important. (LA1)

One of the interviewees (PI3) said that his state department was already using a PSC. However, there were some notable differences between their model and the much maligned UK version. Firstly, the comparison is usually between a PPP and a DB approach as opposed to a PPP and traditional procurement. Secondly, the risk allocation is more equitable between each of the approaches. The UK model was criticised as under PPPs the private sector was seen to be taking on more risk, and when this was given a value and included in the PSC, traditional procurement tended to be more expensive. Thirdly, the state calculates its own discount rate rather than using some mandatory central one. A further criticism of the UK's PSC was that the discount rate set by HMT was too high. Therefore the long-term costs under the PPP model had a lower present value, giving it an unfair advantage over traditional procurement, where all the costs are up front. Another interviewee confirmed the slightly ad hoc nature of VFM analysis in the USA:

> There is no central driving force behind VFM and every state operates its own system. In a lot of cases this is quite loose or reliant on consultants. However, it is important to have some systematic and auditable process that can be looked at by outside parties and which makes the analysis more transparent. (A4)

This interviewee went on to say that it would be beneficial if some central body looked at the different approaches that states take and analysed the non-trivial differences. However, the interviewee would be very surprised if a central organisation (like HMT in the UK) drew up some kind of methodology to be used nationwide as it would be extremely difficult to get widespread adoption of any guidelines. An interesting point was made by one interviewee regarding a novel PPP.

> PPPs aren't necessarily about money. The private sector can create VFM just by being willing to share their expertise in certain areas for the good of the community. (MA1)

The PPP being referred to here is a partnership for public service between police forces and private businesses. The latter group liaise with the police about doing things differently and assist in areas such as resource allocation, leadership development, organisational transformation, human resources policies, problem-solving, leveraging technology and new business strategies. Other arrangements involve large corporate retailers participating in the development of crime prevention strategies and providing assistance to at-risk juveniles. Furthermore, in some communities corporations have helped ensure that non-profit police foundations are set up and run properly so that the public can donate funds and provide assistance to local police departments. The idea behind the PPP is that both sides play a part in creating safe communities, which benefits everyone. A final comment was as follows:

> In my mind VFM isn't about whether or not the public sector can borrow cheaper, it is about getting a large number of projects on the table to make it viable for the private sector to get involved in PPPs. (A5)

Quality of Design of PPP Asset

This was seen as a major benefit of going down the PPP route and was generally deemed to be very important:

> When the public and private sectors work together, we always achieve a better outcome. (C2)
>
> This is vital and it is crucial that the private sector gets it right. If they don't design the road with the long-term in mind, then the road is going to need more maintenance and that means cars can't travel on it. No cars, no toll fees. (O1)
>
> I would say the commitment to maintenance from the private sector is one of the most important aspects of a PPP and design plays a part in that. (C4)

In this case design would include issues such as keeping the road well drained so that adverse weather conditions don't affect traffic flow and also getting the congestion pricing right. The variable toll system is very common in the USA, whereby drivers pay higher tolls at peak times. The lifecycle costs were also relevant in other areas:

Defence PPPs bring all the disparate suppliers under one roof. This means there is a much better appreciation of lifecycle costs, which leads to both savings and less obsolescence. (PI1)

Aesthetic Qualities of PPP Asset

This question is normally more relevant to PPPs where an asset is created, which is inspiring to those who work in it or are the main users. For example, the aesthetics of a newly built school can inspire both teachers and pupils. However, this factor was seen as important in transportation and redevelopment PPPs:

> They can have a role to play. For example, if the contractor provides a clean, vibrant rest area with competitively priced food and good facilities then people may use the PPP road more than an alternative route. (PM1)
>
> It is crucial that a road fits in with its local environment, so aesthetics are important. Due to the cost savings gained by speeding up the construction phase, private contractors have surplus funds to spend on making the road and surrounding area more attractive. (LA1)
>
> If you consider urban redevelopment, aesthetics can really play a part. If features such as attractive benches are put in an area it can lead to more people visiting and staying there and so gradually the footfall increases. (C4)

Innovation

The use of technology and innovation in general were seen to be highly important in assuring project success:

> There are all sorts on innovations that the private sector can bring to a PPP highway project: electronic tolling systems, which save money and improve traffic flow; intelligent transport systems; concrete monitoring systems; and sensors that can detect hairline cracks in bridges. The private sector is more up to date with technological developments that can lead to better maintenance and fewer accidents and are more incentivised to use them. (A3)
>
> PPPs have led to greater collaborations in the production of new and highly effective weapons systems. Moreover, the public partners have learnt how to use quality techniques, such as 'Six Sigma', through working with private-sector companies. (PI1)
>
> Public-sector employees are not incentivised to be innovative; this makes them conservative and resistant to change. However, potential budget deficits have made them turn to PPPs and private-sector innovation. (PI2)

However, innovation is not just about technology:

> I see innovation in PPPs working in three ways—technology, financing and management. (BID1)

One interviewee answered by considering the PPP process:

> I am not sure the private sector is particularly innovative when it comes to PPPs. There are so many models out there now, such as BIDS and TIRZs, so they can just follow them. Sometimes innovation can come from the public sector as well—look at what is happening in Quincy. (C4)

The PPP referred to was initiated by the mayor of Quincy, Massachusetts, and involves the city's redevelopment. Instead of doing this piece by piece the developer will clear 50 acres in the city's centre and then build $300 million of new infrastructure and $1.3 billion of retail, entertainment venues, offices, hotels, parking and housing. Apart from the approach to redevelopment the other novel factor about the deal is that the developer will pay up front for the public improvements, thereby assuming almost all of the financial risk. Only when the infrastructure is finished will Quincy step in and assume responsibility for the debt by issuing general obligation bonds. With those bonds as a guarantee, the developer expects to tap equity and debt markets in order to continue with the redevelopment (Newcombe, 2011).

Another was a little more cynical:

> I think innovation is one of the goals of PPPs at the outset as it is assumed the private partner will bring in a different way of doing things. However, I am not sure this has actually happened in reality. (RSP1)

This last point is of interest as PPPs in health care in the USA are often sold on the basis of the public finance of private innovation and efficiency.

Improved Public-Sector Staff Morale

This was not such an issue in the USA, as it tends to be associated with teaching and medical personnel being motivated by newer facilities with state-of-the-art equipment in PPP schools and hospitals. However, one interviewee did bring up a problem that was often an issue during early PFI projects in the UK.

> Public-sector morale will often be lower if the PPP results in them losing benefits such as pension entitlements if they move to a private-sector firm. (A2)

The Transfer of Undertakings (Protection of Employment) Regulations that were passed in 2006 gave greater protection to public-sector employees in the UK who moved to a private company as a result of a PPP. Another interviewee underlined an unfortunate outcome of PPP efficiencies:

> Saving money often means reducing government personnel who are no longer required. Unfortunately in an economic downturn there are not many places for them to go. (PI1)

As will be seen in Chapter Nine, the prospect of a large number of public employees losing their jobs due to PPPs can cause opposition from unions and reluctance on behalf of politicians to go ahead with projects.

Improved Public Service Delivery

This is seen as a highly important factor by all interviewees; indeed many believe it is what PPPs were all about. Some comments are as follows:

> This is highly important. Putting it simply the public sector cannot do what the private sector can do in some areas, so it makes sense to use them. (NGO1)
> Yes, this is important—particularly when it comes to quality. (RSP1)
> The use of PPPs in defence contracts has meant that weapons and weapons systems have got to where they are meant to be at the right time to a far greater degree than they did in the past. (PI1)

Another interviewee (MA1) described a PPP that doesn't necessarily improve an existing public service, but replaces it once it is decommissioned. This happened in July 2010 in Brooklyn, New York, where unprofitable city bus routes were replaced with privately operated van services. It was felt this was necessary as in certain areas of the city large-scale public transportation was no longer feasible. City officials therefore established the PPP to maintain transit operations along downsized routes. One benefit is a potential reduction in fares by $0.25. However, some community groups have raised concerns about the safety of the vans and the possibility of future privatisation.

Quick Tender Process

PPPs are often seen as taking a long time to get to the construction phase due to a prolonged bidding process; however, in general the interviewees think this is not necessarily a bad thing:

> This is important, but attention must be paid to detail (NGO1)

> I don't see this as being particularly important. You must get the contract right and this can take a long time. (RSP1)

However, one interviewee finds the PPP process a lot quicker:

> In the past we reckoned on two years to get the tender process completed; with a PPP we did it in seven months. (PI2)

Good Project Management

One of the major criticisms of PPPs is that they are not monitored and controlled properly by the public sector, and therefore the private sector gradually lets performance standards slip. However, most interviewees saw project management from the perspective of the contractor:

> This is one thing the private sector is particularly good at and projects get implemented without the usual political wrangling. They have a more bottom-line oriented approach, which means that things get done faster and more efficiently. (LA1)
>
> Under PPPs work in progress and inventories in general have been reduced, supply chains have been sped up and the availability of fully functional weapons systems has been increased. This is all down to effective project management on behalf of the private partners. (PI1)
>
> This is important as under PPPs more demands are made of the private partner and they run projects better. (RSP1)

However, one interviewee highlighted changes one state made that had improved the contractor's performance:

> It is important that the public partner monitors the contract correctly. Since our department implemented a more focused performance measurement system, the construction on-time performance has improved from 20% to 90% and the construction on-budget performance has improved from 51% to 90%. (PM1)

Good Working Relationships between All Parties

PPPs are seen to work when there is a collaborative relationship between the various partners, and there was a general agreement that this is an important factor:

> I would say this is the most important factor out of all of those mentioned. At the end of the day you have to get on professionally with the companies you are working with. (RSP1)

This is important, especially when there may not be an immediate return for the private-sector party. (NGO1)

This is essential. If the relationship becomes adversarial then both parties will lose out as a tit-for-tat mentality can build up. (A3)

Profit for the Private-Sector Party

Whist some see profit as a dirty word when it is associated with public service delivery, the private sector will not get involved in PPPs if they are not going to get some return. The interviewees had no issues with regard to the private sector making a profit:

There are those who will always believe that the private profit motive is incompatible with public service delivery, but they are missing the point. If the private sector can provide a more efficient service, at a lower cost, and still make a profit then everyone benefits. (C2)

The private sector has a profit motive; it is up to the public partner to incentivise them to realise that profit through enhanced performance. (PI1)

The first thing you must realise when you are sitting down to negotiate with the private sector is that they are there to make a profit. (PI3)

In most cases the private sector is looking to make some sort of return and at the end of the day that is why they exist in the first place. I am not against profit when it is linked to innovation—especially when people's livelihoods are involved. (NGO1)

This interviewee worked in an organisation that was involved in the improvement of lives in developing nations and had a large number of PPPs in operation. As far as the USA end of the operations are concerned, this organisation forms PPPs with a number of high-profile, private-sector, for-profit organisations, including those in the IT sector (software systems development and applications), oil companies and sports companies. Normally these large organisations provide assistance through two main arms. The first is through the foundations they have formed; these have charitable status and are seen as purely philanthropic. However, the other way they provide assistance is through their normal corporate operations. In such cases, whilst they are giving some of their services or products for free, they are looking for some sort of commercial return. In some situations it is simply marketing or brand awareness; in others there is a particular item they are wishing to sell to either the governments or the people in the countries being helped—for example, registration or licence fees for software, and certification fees for certain educational programmes.

The two arms of these private organisations are kept quite separate. The foundation money is ring-fenced and companies are careful not to attempt to obtain any marketing or other commercial benefit from any funding.

However, the corporate arm has more of a predatory outlook and people working within the NGO are always aware that the funding could be withdrawn at any moment. This is not the attitude of all organisations and at least one CEO has stated that he is committed to working with them for the long term. The interviewee went on to state that sometimes the CEOs of these companies wish for nothing more than just a positive association when the people in these countries think of them. This isn't quite the same as brand awareness as the products will not necessarily ever be sold in a particular country.

Another comment about private-sector profit is as follows:

> We work in partnership with mainly non-profit private organisations but also with some for-profits. However, just because an organisation is classed as not-for-profit it doesn't prevent their CEOs leaving with million-dollar golden parachutes. It just means any surplus funds don't go to shareholders. Nevertheless, I would say these organisations are trying to make sure they don't lose money, rather than focussing on the size of their profit. (RSP1)

This interviewee, who worked in the health sector, talked about two recent PPPs. The first was a nationwide PPP known as Partnership for Patients, the aims of which are to bring about a 40% reduction in preventable hospital-acquired conditions over three years (i.e., 1.8 million fewer injuries and 60,000 lives saved) and a 20% reduction in 30-day readmissions in three years (i.e., 1.6 million patients recover without readmission). This has the potential to save $35 billion in three years. The other PPP is known as the Measure Applications Partnership, which has the aim of selecting quality measures for public reporting, payment and other programmes in the health sector.

Reduction of Public-Sector Costs

This is seen as one of the major benefits of PPPs: using the greater efficiencies of the private sector to reduce the costs of public service delivery. Some of the comments are as follows:

> I would say this is one of the most important aspects. The use of PPPs in defence logistics led to huge savings for the DoD as well as a far greater performance. (PI1)
>
> In a PPP project everyone focuses on the construction costs, but the operation and maintenance costs can often amount to a lot more. Under a PPP the private sector is committed to these over the life of the contract and this saves the public sector a lot of money. (PI3)
>
> Yes, this is very important. The public sector must save money due to the PPP. (RSP1)

If they bring about social benefits this leads to a reduction in social costs, which tend to be borne by the public. (A1)

It is important, but I would say as long as public benefits increase and costs don't go up, then the PPP has been successful. (C2)

One of the main reasons we went in for a PPP was to drive down costs. (PI2)

The PPP the last interviewee was involved in is very interesting. A large metro economy was looking to reduce the costs of collecting transit fares. Traditionally this had been conducted via machines that took cash, but the costs of handling this cash were increasing. Furthermore, the process slows down customers and there can be problems with dirty or damaged notes. The city's transportation authority decided to go for a card-based system, in which customers could use credit, debit or prepaid cards. The latter were essential for those customers who did not have bank accounts. The company that eventually won the bid bore all capital costs and was not seeking any repayment by the transportation authority. This was because the idea was sold to them on the basis of a marketing opportunity. A huge number of customers would have their first experience of contactless technology and associate it with the brand of the winning bidder. The model chosen was BOT, with the facility returning to the city in ten years. Moreover, whilst the company takes a percentage of the revenue, minimum and maximum parameters have been set; therefore it is also bearing some demand risk.

Fewer Administrative Duties for Public-Sector Senior Personnel

This factor may again be more relevant to PPPs which result in a school, hospital or prison being built and where the day-to-day running of the facility is handed over to the private sector. Under such an agreement the person in charge (e.g., the school principal) can focus more on core tasks and less on administration. Nevertheless, one interviewee saw it as an important issue:

This is a very important factor in the health sector. Most facilities are understaffed or have personnel without sufficient competences. Hiring the right number of adequately qualified staff takes time and would create a lot of extra work for managers. Contracting staff via PPPs is a much easier way to solve these problems. (RSP1)

Transfer of Risk to Most Appropriate Party

Although some literature stresses the importance of risk transfer to the most appropriate party (see, for example, Geddes, 2011), the interviewees did not see risk as a major concern and there seemed to be more of a focus on costs. Although some risks, with which a UK audience would be familiar, such as demand and construction, are considered when contracts are being drawn up, there appeared to be a far greater emphasis on financial risks. One of the respondents outlined some of these:

> In a concession arrangement it is essential that the public sector places the correct value on the asset, or else the public will be short-changed. Moreover, there is the risk that in order to pay for an asset the financial burden is passed on to future generations due to budget tricks. (MA1)

In both cases these are more risks of PPPs in general and are not relevant to the transfer of risk to the most appropriate party in a specific contract. However, one interviewee believes one risk is often overlooked:

> You have also got to consider what I would call sovereign risk, and that is if some state goes back on the terms of the contract. This is why I can never understand the outcry when a foreign company bids for a PPP contract. They are always going to bear this risk. (A3)

Whilst A4 agreed with this point, he or she stated that there was growing political opposition to returns being made via US infrastructure leaving the country as the asset was foreign-owned. This lack of emphasis on risk transfer, particularly when compared to the UK, was explained by two interviewees:

> People don't know how to price risk very well or who ought to bear what. Risk must be priced accurately or private companies won't be sufficiently hurt if they walk away from a project. There has not been much work in risk transfer in the USA, but there really ought to be more. Agencies should be prepared to pay for proper longitudinal research, so when a project matures someone can state whether it worked or not. (A5)
>
> I think there a general misunderstanding of what risk transfer actually is, with people seeing it as mainly a political issue. However, if one looks at the San Diego's South Bay Expressway, which went bankrupt, it was the private sector that lost money and the taxpayer was not affected. So the risk taken on by the private sector is very real. (LA1)

The company behind the South Bay Expressway filed for bankruptcy in March 2010 following a legal dispute with the road's builders and less toll revenue than expected. As a result, around $200 million in shareholder equity was written off (Toll Road News, 2010). The expressway could not have opened at a worse time as it coincided with the subprime-mortgage crisis in Southern California. Expected housing developments were cancelled, and recession-battered motorists turned to neighbouring freeways. Therefore traffic was about half of what investors had expected. Another interviewee (PF1) also stated that the government in the USA does not underwrite any of the private loans for infrastructure projects.

One interviewee stated that the correct balance is important:

> You have to incentivise the private partner as that is how improvements come about, but in order to encourage private-sector participation you don't want to transfer so much risk that it is not worth their while. (RSP1)

Another interviewee questioned the whole concept of risk transfer:

> Although things have improved in the past five years with more risk transfer or sharing, the private sector still tends to get a better deal. I don't think that PPPs should be based solely on risk transfer as the natural position of a private company is to try and minimise risk. (A4)

However, one state department had an approach to risk that is very similar to that of the UK:

> We do a complete identification and quantification of any risks as well as calculating the likelihood of them occurring. Once we have done this risk profile we sit down with our contractors and advisors and allocate the risks to the most appropriate partner. For example, there is no point in shifting a hidden hazard risk to the private sector as they will place a large cost on it and it might never materialise. (PI3)

The interviewees were also asked if they think there are any other factors that are important to the success of a PPP. Two believe that overcoming public opposition is crucial, with A1 stating that there is always great public participation in the USA whenever groups are formed around an issue that could have an impact on a locality. A5 mentioned some development schemes he worked on in another role. These took place around railway stations in a suburban area of a major city (such PPPs will be looked at in more detail in Chapter Eight). Opposition came both from local people who did not want to live amongst the nexus of development and from some area officials who did not want the area to become more urbanised. The next series of questions looks at a number of potential drawbacks with PPPs that could limit the overall success of a project. Once again the interviewees were asked how significant they think these are.

Less Flexibility in Public-Sector Budgets

This is due to the fact that under a PPP money is ring-fenced for certain items and cannot be transferred to other areas if there is a sudden shortfall. Only one interviewee commented on this:

It can be a problem due to the long-term nature of most PPP agreements. In the past the DoD left its readiness accounts highly flexible so they could use the money for other areas. This is no longer possible under long-term contracts. However, what does the DoD value more? Having weapons in the right place at the right time, whilst saving money, or having more flexibility in their budgets? (PI1)

A readiness account is an operational and maintenance account, which in reality is used to fund a wide range of military activities. The foregoing point is often made in relation to how public-sector budgets have been used in the past to focus on short-term emergencies, as opposed to the maintenance of a facility (see also Chapter Two). In the long term the spending is normally much higher as the asset falls into disrepair. PPP agreements therefore can force public-sector managers to think of different ways of coping with short-term problems, as they no longer have the option of taking money out of maintenance budgets.

Contract Too Rigid

The lack of flexibility in contracts can sometimes lead to frustration on behalf of the public-sector partner. For example, there have been stories of schools which had to call contractors in for simple maintenance tasks that a member of staff could have carried out in a matter of minutes. This was not seen as major issue:

> This can be a problem and again it is all down to experience in the public sector when it comes to contract management. I think that if problems are addressed as they arise and both parties have a flexible approach, then this can be eliminated. (A3)

One interviewee believes the contractor suffered more from a lack of flexibility:

> This is always an issue; however there are so many rules that it will be hard to change. (RSP1)

Time-Consuming Process

Such a factor could include the bidding and subsequent negotiation process and the time-consuming nature of dealing with contractors for day-to-day operational issues. Again it was not seen as a major issue:

> This is a factor, but it has to be this way as it is so important to get the contract right. (RSP1)

Limited Information Available

Some UK PPP projects have been associated with a lack of transparency and accountability. Whilst some interviewees disagree with this viewpoint, others believe a certain amount of confidentiality is necessary:

> I would say that PPP projects are more transparent than those run by the state. There are benchmarks, performance standards and indicators—all of which must be adhered to by the contractor. If something goes wrong you know who is to blame. In the old days when something went wrong, even a fatal accident caused by lousy infrastructure, no one was accountable and no one lost their job. (PPPA1)
>
> There is a total lack of transparency in public-sector policy-making. (PI2)
>
> I think you almost have a clash of cultures here: by its very nature, private decision-making is not always open and transparent, and yet the appropriate use of public resources and the appropriate distribution of publicly generated benefits are key public considerations. (C2)
>
> Although greater transparency is always an aim of any government, one has to be careful when considering PPP projects. The process must be kept as competitive as possible and this will not be the case if information is released about other bids. (A3)

Another interviewee agreed with this point, but believes that doesn't negate the need for transparency:

> As long as the process, from beginning to end, is as open as possible, then it isn't necessary to give away competitive details about bidding companies. (C2)

PROFITS NOT SHARED BETWEEN ALL PARTIES

Some of the early UK PPP projects reaped huge financial gains that were not shared with the public partner. Moreover, some projects were refinanced again resulting in unshared gains. In the UK there is a now a far more equitable arrangement with regard to profit sharing, and in the current climate refinancing as a method of easy profit is highly unlikely. The comments reflect a slightly different attitude in the USA:

> Profit-sharing clauses are now more common in contracts. However, if one is included the private partner might put in a smaller up-front contribution. (LA1)
>
> Again it all comes down to incentives; if there is going to be too much sharing of profits then the private partner will not participate. (RSP1)

One interviewee discussed how his or her organisation's profit-sharing arrangements work:

> We work on a system of revenue bands. Up to a certain level of revenue for the contractor there is no profit sharing, but as they reach certain revenue levels the amount shared with us increases. (PI3)

Inexperience of Public Sector at Contract Negotiations

Although PPPs have been going for some time, the type of project that results in infrastructure being built is still fairly new to the USA. This means public-sector personnel need to rapidly develop an expertise in areas such as the screening of bidders, contract negotiation, contract monitoring and is some cases contract renegotiation (Geddes, 2011). This lack of experience in such areas was acknowledged as a serious problem, but changes are under way:

> This is of the utmost importance as public-sector officials are taking on roles that they are not familiar with and if they don't fulfil those roles properly taxpayers' money can be wasted. Even though it might be costly, until proper expertise is built up officials should not be afraid to seek outside assistance. It is vital that these contracts are drawn up correctly. (A3)
>
> One of the most important aspects of trying to broker a deal with the private sector is timing. You have to know when the maximum amount of funding can be leveraged from a local business or property developer. This is a skill that is lacking in the public sector. (TA1)
>
> If the public sector doesn't write the contract correctly they can be taken to the cleaners. They have to be a smart as the private sector. (MA1)
>
> The GAO recently noted that whilst the USDOT has done much to promote the benefits of PPPs it needs to do more. This will hopefully lead to the creation of dedicated PPP units which can fulfil functions such as quality control, policy formulation and coordination, technical advice, standardization and dissemination and promotion of PPPs. So far only a handful of states have set up such units and some of these are not totally dedicated to PPPs. (C1)
>
> The assistance available to states is growing; there is an advisory body within central government which provides technical assistance, the NCSL provides legal and financial advice on PPPs to all sectors and there are various bodies that come under USDOT that can help. (LA1)

However, it is not an issue for some interviewees:

> Both sides know what they are doing. In many cases we are working with fixed price contracts so there is less leeway for the private partner. (RSP1)

> I think it depends on the background of the employees. I came from a finance background so I had a lot of experience with contracts. (PI2)

Another public-sector interviewee also comes from a private background—indeed his or her whole team does:

> There are nine people working here and all have worked in the private sector in various roles. So we have people with legal, financial and engineering expertise, for example. But we are all still learning and for the huge contracts we are taking on I need to augment this with up-to-date, external expertise. But this is a flexible resource—I use it and pay for it as I need it. (PI3)

This final point about the use of consultants is often overlooked, and when factors such as holiday pay and pension entitlements are taken into consideration they can work out a lot cheaper than hiring extra staff. This interviewee also stressed that any fee levels are capped at the outset so that huge bills are not run up by consultants prolonging certain activities. However, TA1 made the valid point that any consultant still has to be managed, which is a skill not all public employees have.

The interviewees were then asked some more general questions.

Dos and Don'ts

The aim of this question was to ascertain what advice the interviewees would give to those embarking on the PPP process or how they believe the scheme could be improved. Several of the responses seem to indicate that the USA, despite its long history of PPPs, is still coming to terms with how to approach infrastructure projects. What is also clear is the importance of legislation:

> The federal government has a part to play and they need to make sure that the private sector is both fully committed to PPPs and has an understanding of the public interest. (A2)
>
> PPPs can be a valuable tool for states when they are developed by the executive and legislative branches in a collaborative atmosphere. Moreover, the public must be involved. It is critical that elected officials educate themselves and the public when considering PPPs as opposed to traditional procurement. Solid enabling legislation is the key to thorough consideration and success of PPP projects. (PA1)
>
> A legislative framework is essential, as is investor confidence. (LA1)
>
> When PPP legislation comes on the agenda of any state, it gives an opportunity for various stakeholders to make their views known and raise any concerns. This can lead to fewer objections further down the line. (A3)

A statutory foundation for the implementation of each partnership strengthens the hand of the public partner and thus negates many of the common drawbacks associated with PPPs. (PPPA1)

There needs to be a model, which all PPP projects can follow. If they are not following that model then they should not be classified as a PPP, but as contracting out or something else. (A1)

An interesting point is made by Geddes (2011), who calls for consistency in a government's treatment of private investment to create what could be called policy predictability. Such a stable regulatory environment could lead to reduced transaction costs as the contracts would become more standardised and therefore less time-consuming to draw up. BID1 also commented about the uncertainty caused by mayoral elections every four years. The newly elected mayor may appoint new officials to key positions, and this can lead to PPPs being put on hold or even cancelled after considerable private involvement. This can make the private sector wary of entering into deals that will have lengthy negotiation periods. A change of governor can also lead to a different attitude towards PPPs. For example, according to A5, in California Arnold Schwarzenegger was in favour of them, and despite political opposition persevered so that the Presidio Parkway PPP finally went ahead. However, his successor is not in favour of PPPs and progress in this area has now stalled. The comments regarding public involvement made by PA1 will be expanded upon in Chapter Nine.

There are some other, more general comments:

You must know who you are working with and never neglect them as a partner. (NGO1)

The incentives for the private partner have to be right. Moreover, it is important to try and streamline the process whilst always being aware of accountability. (RSP1)

There is currently a lack of targeted metrics, at the federal and state level, to analyse projects and conduct impact assessments. Therefore good projects have been missed that would have had measurable economic effect. Institutions are also siloed and compartmentalised, preventing learning on how to structure, implement and finance projects across different sectors. This is especially important for multi-modal projects that do not fit a specific mould for a traditional infrastructure project. These issues need to be addressed. (C1)

Finally a point that is often overlooked was made:

There is a tendency to blame a poorly conceived idea on the PPP model. When projects go wrong there is a tendency to point the finger at PPPs in general. A PPP cannot rescue a flawed concept. (C2)

Are PPPs More Accepted in the USA Than They Are in the UK?

A lot of the interviewees made the valid point that they are not aware how acceptable PPPs are in the UK, but there were still some interesting comments made:

> I think that we (in the USA) see the limitations of government more and feel that any innovation is going to come from the private sector. (NGO1)
>
> There is a great private-sector involvement in health provision in the USA. In fact traditionally they were the main provider, so I don't think people object to PPPs in this sector. Moreover, there is a certain distrust of government in this country. (RSP1)
>
> People generally think that the government is not very good and that if you want something done the private sector is more likely to do it. Plus nobody has a problem with the private sector making a profit by delivering public services. (C4)
>
> People tend to trust the US private sector, but are more wary when there is foreign investment into a PPP. Yet there have been some very good deals made with Spanish and Australian companies. (PI3)

This interviewee went on to say that when he was discussing urban redevelopment options with representatives from the public sector in Turin, Italy, they could not contemplate the private sector taking on as great a role as they do in the USA in this area. There was a feeling the public would not accept them making a profit from an activity seen as coming under the aegis of the state. One interviewee thinks the situation is more ambivalent:

> It really depends on the project and to a certain extent the state. Areas such as parking garages may as well be run by the private sector, yet there is less agreement when it comes to its involvement in schools, for example. I always feel there are some real 'can do' states when it comes to PPPs—for example, Virginia, Texas and Colorado—but other states are more hesitant. (C1)

This interviewee referred to a poll undertaken by Lazard (2010), a global financial advisory and asset management organisation, which found that there was a high political acceptability for the private sector to get involved with roads and bridges, airports, public transportation systems, convention centres and stadiums, parking garages and waste disposal and recycling, but low acceptability for its involvement in the state lottery, ports and waterways, drinking water systems and wastewater treatment facilities. Finally, there are conflicting views over how PPPs are viewed by the political parties:

> I am not sure they are more accepted. I would say there are two camps. Firstly there are those that think the government should be responsible

for the provision of all public services; then there are those that say if the provision can be improved or carried out more cheaply by the private sector then they should do it. Interestingly these two camps do not divide along political lines. (A1)

I think Republicans are more inclined to use PPPs, whist Democrats are against them as they believe in the collective good and feel that lower socio-economic groups can suffer when the private sector gets involved in public service delivery. (PI2)

This last interviewee went on to say that there was recent groundswell of opinion against PPPs, but this was mainly down to campaigns by certain journalists and politicking. This interviewee also believes the number one problem facing the USA is a lack of leadership in public agencies, which could lead to poor decisions being made and a mistrust of the private sector based on irrational considerations.

CONCLUSIONS

Some of the foregoing comments echo those made by the cheerleaders of PPPs all over the world: they drive down costs due to competition and greater efficiencies; they improve the delivery of a public service; they consider the lifecycle costs of an asset; they increase the supply of capital; the superior skills of the private sector are leveraged; greater innovation comes via the private sector; and projects are completed quicker. Other remarks concerning them being just one approach to service delivery and not being appropriate in all sectors have also been made many times before. However, a lot of issues that are of concern in the UK are not as important in the USA. In some cases this may be down to the fact that apart from transportation, redevelopment and defence PPPs, new assets are not necessarily created due to the arrangement. Therefore, factors such as the improved morale of public-sector employees, fewer administrative duties for senior personnel, the rigidity of the contract and less flexibility in budgets are not major concerns.

There is also less concern about the profit for the private partner, the long tender process and transparency. With regard to the former the interviewees see nothing wrong with the private sector making a profit from public service delivery, and many stated that was why they entered into PPPs in the first place. However, there are cases when the return comes from less tangible factors such as brand awareness and public relations. In some instances the tender process was actually shorter with a PPP, and where this didn't occur it wasn't considered as a problem as the main consideration was to get the contract right. Transparency is generally seen to be greater under PPPs and where it isn't it is due to the competitive nature of the process. Moreover, government at all levels is considered to be very secretive when it comes to decision-making. Project management is generally felt to be of a high standard and this is down to getting the incentives and key performance indicators (KPIs) right in the first place. However, if anything, the public sector in the USA was seen as being poorer at contract negotiations than that in other countries, including the UK. It also appears that profit sharing is not as regulated in the USA.

Two major areas of controversy in UK PPPs, risk transfer and VFM, are not currently major issues in the USA. Indeed, there is a general feeling that VFM analyses are carried out on a fairly ad hoc basis. However, tools such as the much-criticised PSC are being considered to improve VFM and are already in use in some states. Likewise, whilst some states conduct thorough risk profiles for projects, generally financial risk seems to be the dominant issue. When asked about what countries have influenced the development of PPPs in the USA, it was clear that they are currently looking overseas for ideas. As well as the PSC, the practices of the UK (and other countries) such as setting up dedicated PPP units and more private finance are also being adopted or considered. The USA is also trying to ensure that PPP-enabling legislation is adopted by as many states as possible, and, whilst states seem to have almost total autonomy when it comes to using PPPs, central guidance and funding are still seen as important.

Finally, PPPs do seem to be more acceptable in the USA and this is down to a general distrust and disregard of government. Decision-making at all levels of governance appears to be dogged by politicking and irrational decision-making, and it is felt that the private sector can do a better job in most areas. Traditionally the private sector has always been involved in public service delivery and their profit motive is not as suspect as it would be in the UK. However, one interviewee believes that this is beginning to change, although the anti–private-sector sentiment is often based on misinformation. Furthermore, opposition to the foreign ownership of infrastructure assets remains high, despite such firms bearing sovereign risk and generally bringing both expertise and funding into the USA. The next chapter looks at four specific PPP projects in the Washington, DC area.

8 Public-Private Partnerships in Operation

This chapter outlines four specific PPPs either under consideration or in operation in the Washington, DC area. Due to the dominance of transportation in PPP projects, both in terms of overall spending and as an issue that was of a particular poignancy when the author was in the USA, two of these come under this sector. These are the I-95 High Occupancy Toll (HOT) lane project and the extension of Washington, DC's Metrorail line to Dulles International Airport, both of which are being purchased by the Virginia Department of Transportation (VDOT). The Metrorail case study also looks at other stations on the network and how they have been financed. The other two PPPs come under the banner of economic development or urban regeneration, but in one case could also be seen as having a social benefit for the surrounding area and therefore lowering social costs for the state or local government. These are Union Station in Washington, DC and the Inner Harbor area in Baltimore. The information for these case studies was gathered via a combination of interviews, observation and secondary research.

TRANSPORTATION

In 2011 there was tremendous pressure on the key decision makers in the USA to both kick-start a faltering economy and improve the unemployment figures. One of the best ways to go about this was seen to be via large-scale construction projects. One of the most pressing areas appeared to be that of transportation, with what was generally seen as a crumbling infrastructure, excessive traffic congestion and an outdated system of funding. PPPs were seen as a solution to these various problems (see, for example, Engel et al., 2011; Geddes, 2011).

If the UK's PFI type of arrangement is used as a basis of comparison, the actual use of PPPs in transportation is relatively small in the USA. This is demonstrated in Table 8.1.

As can be seen, Europe dominates this sector of the PPP market, with the USA making up only 7% of the global figure. This equates to about $36.4 billion worth of PPP projects. Over this period 92 PPP transportation

Table 8.1   Road and Rail PPPs Worldwide, Nominal Total Cost, 1985–2010 (Public Works Financing (PWF), 2010)

Region	Percentage of Total Cost
Europe	46
Asia and Australia	26
Mexico, the Caribbean and Latin America	16
USA	7
Canada	3
Africa and the Middle East	2

projects have taken place in the USA (PWF, 2010), although this number includes DB projects which are not included in Table 8.1. Most of these (81% both in terms of number of projects and value) are for highways, bridges and tunnels, and the rest are for rail projects. The exception is the construction of the International Air Terminal at John F. Kennedy Airport in New York, which is the only airport PPP project. Out of these projects the DB form of PPP has been used the most in the USA (63% in number and 46% in value). The more complex DBFO model (including maintenance of the facility) has historically been used less (13% in number and 27% in value) but is starting to grow in popularity (PWF, 2010).

According to one of the interviewees (PF1) a real problem exists in the Midwest of the USA, where roads are heavily used due to the constant east-west traffic and are subsequently falling into disrepair. The problem is that these states have lost their ability to raise sufficient taxes due to the lack of industry and subsequent employment. Moreover, the roads are not currently tolled, so it could be difficult to generate any private interest. In general, PPP transportation projects are found in the largest metro economies, with Dallas, Los Angeles, New York, Washington, DC, Miami and Chicago among the top ten metros in terms of the value of their PPPs. Geddes (2011) states that the Washington, DC region in general and North Virginia in particular are amongst the fastest-growing areas in the USA. Traffic congestion in the area is rife and there have been ever-growing demands for solutions to this problem. Congestion leads to a variety of problems, including lost productivity, a non-constructive use of time, a waste of a finite resource (fuel), air pollution and general driver frustration and anxiety. The area has used PPPs for road projects before, with the Dulles Greenway and I-495/Washington, DC Beltway HOT lanes being two major projects. A HOT lane is where a variable toll is charged (depending on the time of day or level of congestion) to any driver wishing to avoid traffic jams. They are distinct from a high-occupancy vehicle (HOV) lane, which encourages carpooling. With a HOV lane, any car with three occupants can travel free. This has led to an informal system known as 'slugging', in which people queue up at certain locations in order to share rides with what could be total strangers. Environmentalists (although clearly against car usage per se) prefer HOV lanes to HOT lanes as they state that the latter lead to what are known as 'Lexus lanes'. This is where affluent drivers, who do not wish to share their car with strangers, are not put off by the high fees and will use the HOT lanes as a means of avoiding congestion.

I-95 HOV/HOT LANES

I-95 is the main highway on the east coast of the USA and runs parallel to the Atlantic Ocean from Florida to Maine. It serves some of the most populated urban areas in the country, including Miami, Richmond, Washington, Philadelphia, New York and Boston, and is the longest north-south route of the interstate highway system. As it comes into Washington, I-95 joins with the aforementioned DC Beltway before heading northwards towards Baltimore. It is therefore an integral part of Washington's roadway system. At the time of writing a substantial amount of construction had recently been carried out on I-95 in the DC area, including work on the interchange between it and the DC Beltway and six miles of road and bridge widening. The I-95 HOV/HOT lanes PPP has been proposed as a means of further reducing traffic congestion in the DC area. The original proposal was shortened following a lawsuit by Arlington County that prevented the HOT lanes extending through that region as well as the nearby city of Alexandria. As a result the project will consist of a 29-mile, as opposed to a 35-mile, highway between Garrisonville Road in Stafford County (which lies to the southwest of Washington) and Edsall Road, just north of the DC Beltway.

The project now consists of three sets of improvements to the current I-95: adding nine miles of new lanes; improving the existing HOV lanes by creating or upgrading access points at key interchanges; and increasing the existing HOV lanes from two to three lanes. Although VDOT will continue to have ownership and oversight of the road, the project is being financed by a mixture of private and public money. Private money is coming from Fluor Virginia (part of the Fluor Corporation) and Transurban DRIVe LLC (Transurban), which, according to a representative from VDOT, are making a substantial investment up front to fund construction of the lanes. Transurban, a toll-road owner and operator with interests in the USA and Australia, will operate and provide routine maintenance for the lanes. The Fluor Corporation is one of the world's largest publicly owned engineering, procurement, construction and maintenance services companies. The breakdown of the required $940 million is as follows: Fluor-Transurban is expected to pay $843 million and the state will contribute $97 million.

Construction is due to begin in the spring of 2012 and the project should take three years to complete. At the DC Beltway the I-95 HOT lanes will connect with another 14-mile HOT lane project currently under construction and due for completion at the end of 2012. The alternative was to widen I-95 in some areas without the financial aid of a PPP. However, funding is in short supply, with the main source of transportation funding still being the gas tax, which is levied at federal, state and, to a lesser extent, local levels. Unfortunately, this no longer produces sufficient revenue. This is due to the fact that, along with the proliferation of more fuel-efficient vehicles and fuels, the USA is witnessing the largest sustained drop in driving that it has ever seen. As a result, people in the USA are consuming much less gasoline and paying less in gas taxes, which is putting less revenue into transportation programmes. In addition, the federal gas tax has not been raised since 1993.

This project has met with a certain amount of resistance, particularly from environmentalists who are putting forward the well-documented argument that building more roads simply leads to more cars using them. There have been suggestions that more park-and-ride schemes would help. There is currently one in operation at Garrisonville, a small community lying about 40 miles to the southwest of Washington and very close to I-95. However, this is full by 7:00 a.m. Other suggestions have included extending the HOV requirements to four people in a car. Under the proposed scheme the HOV principle would still exist, but solo drivers willing to pay for using the lane could now do so. It should also be noted that neither the current HOV lanes nor the proposed HOT lanes are permanent in that they are designated only for certain hours of the day, obviously those when the traffic is heaviest. Another flexible arrangement on some roads in the USA is the reversibility of some lanes. For example, say there is a six-lane highway going into a major city; in the morning four lanes can be used for traffic going into the city, and then the central two can be reversed at some stage in the day, so for the after-work commute there are now four lanes coming out of the city. Other proposals are as follows: Virginia could choose a programme more heavily dependent on buses and trains to reduce congestion; or it could modify land-use planning and encourage telecommuting to reduce the demand for I-95.

The arguments for the HOT lanes are that the private involvement will bring greater incentives to keep the traffic moving (e.g., accidents will be cleared quickly) and also to stop drivers cheating the current system. Less popular will be the move away from letting the owners of the more fuel-efficient hybrid cars use the tolled road for free even if they are travelling alone. Whilst drivers claim that paying tolls on roads amounts to double taxation, the counterclaim from government is that taxes pay for roads and tolls pay for improvements. Moreover, the governor of Virginia at the time, Robert McDonnell, stated that the PPP would provide an economic boost by supporting nearly 8,000 jobs over the construction period and stimulating $2 billion in economic activity (Halsey III, 2011).

VDOT has held a number of public meetings at all stages of this project, including three informational ones in the counties affected by the extended route (Fairfax, Prince William and Stafford counties). The other stages were the environmental assessment and the air quality and noises analyses.

Officials from this department stress that within the confines of confidentiality they have to be transparent with the public. If something is withheld at these public meetings and comes to light later with negative consequences for the community, trust will be lost and any future projects could be subject to more local opposition. These meetings are not just one-way; any concerns are noted and changes can be made as a result of public consultation. However, the environment assessment was described by Stewart Schwartz, the executive director of the Coalition for Smarter Growth, as being completely inadequate (Halsey III, 2011).

DULLES INTERNATIONAL AIRPORT METRORAIL EXTENSION

Washington, DC is served by three airports, Dulles International (Dulles), Baltimore Washington International Thurgood Marshall (BWI) and the Ronald Reagan National (Reagan) Airports. As their names imply the first two are used for a mixture of external and internal flights, whereas the latter is used for internal flights only. BWI Airport is approximately 33 miles from the centre of Washington, Dulles Airport is about 26 miles away and Reagan Airport is closer at roughly six miles from the centre. The latter is also linked to Washington's Metrorail (Metro), which clearly gives tourists and local people more options when travelling to and from the airport. BWI Airport also has a rail connection to Washington via the mainline Amtrak service. However, passengers using Dulles Airport need to use buses, taxis or personal cars to get to and from Washington. As already mentioned, Washington, like most cities in the USA, suffers from severe traffic congestion problems and any initiative that reduces the amount of cars on the road will prove popular with a number of interest groups. The Dulles area has already experienced one PPP transportation project that was not overly successful, the aforementioned (see earlier and Chapter Four) Dulles Greenway.

The project to link Dulles Airport to the city's Metro service has been planned in two phases. The first phase involves the building of an offshoot of the current Orange Line of the Metro to create a Silver Line that will run from East Falls Church in Arlington County to Reston, Virginia (about six miles east of Dulles). This extension to the Metro began in March 2009 and is due to be completed in 2013. The second phase will run from Reston, via Dulles Airport, and on to Loudon County, which lies to the northwest. The two phases will lead to 23 miles of new Metro track and cost in the region of $6 billion. According to a representative from VDOT the Dulles Metro project is a key part of its integrated transportation solution that maximises investments in Metro, buses, carpools, I-495 HOT lanes, the Virginia Railway Express (the state's commuter rail service), road improvements and teleworking. It is also anticipated that this project will encourage residential and commercial transit-oriented development (see ahead and the next two case studies for how this works in practice).

In the summer of 2011 the second phase of the project became hampered by financial disputes when the Metropolitan Washington Airports Authority stated that it wanted more money from both federal and state governments (Hedgpeth, 2011a) to meet the overall cost of $3.5 billion. Some money ($330 million) had been saved due to a decision in July 2011 to locate the Dulles Airport station above ground. However, more was needed and the two Virginia counties which the airport straddles, Loudoun and Fairfax, were trying to help reduce the overall cost by finding a way to pay for parking garages and the Route 28 station by using PPPs or TIFIA loans. The Route 28 station is at the intersection of the Dulles Airport Access Highway/Dulles Toll Road and would be the stop before the airport itself if approaching from Washington. Moreover, in September 2011 phase one was running six months behind schedule. It is due to be completed by August 2013 and in service four months later. Whilst the contractors were confident this lost time could be made up, the projects contingency fund of $300 million was rapidly running out, with only $84 million remaining in September 2011. Eventually a solution for phase two was reached in early November 2011, whereby extra money was promised by both the federal government and the state of Virginia. However, it was clear that what had begun as simply a DB project would subsequently require more complex PPPs for its full completion (Hedgpeth, 2011b). Phase one of the project had used some private money in the form of a special assessment district (see ahead) formed in Fairfax County.

Generally TA1 believes that rail is seen as a poor relation to road when competing for federal or state funding; moreover there are always problems when rail lines (whether over- or underground) cross state or county lines, as areas that did not contribute to new infrastructure, such as a station, could still benefit. A further problem with extensions to the Metro is that pressure is put on the central stations that could subsequently suffer from capacity problems. Nonetheless, investment in the Metro (or other forms of public transport) is seen as essential in order to attract young people to an area, as they will often be burdened with debt from their education and will not be able to afford a car. Moreover, a better Metro network means savings for other citizens who no longer need to own a car, less stressful and quicker journeys as road congestion is avoided and, from a government perspective, no need to keep building more roads. A final reason for investment in transit (as opposed to roads) is what Leinberger and Doherty (2010) refer to as a shift in residential choices from low-density, car-dependent suburbs to walkable city neighbourhoods, where despite the name public transport is still essential. This leads to what is sometimes referred to as the virtuous circle (Levinson and Istrate, 2011); infrastructure creates access, access creates value, value can be captured to finance infrastructure and therefore create further access, and thus value. However, as reported in Chapter Seven, the interviewee A5 mentioned that some communities like their suburban status and don't want to become part of an expanded urban area.

Notwithstanding, as seen in the Dulles Airport extension, money is often a problem, and although value is created in a region when a Metro station is built, it is hard to measure. An innovative solution was used for the funding of the New York Avenue Metro station, which is located quite close to Washington's Union Station (see next set of case studies). Funding of $110 million came from both private and public sectors and included the following:

- $35 million in private funds from area businesses, including $10 million in land; amortised over 30 years;
- $44 million from DC; and
- $31 million from the federal government, including $6 million for the construction of a portion of the Metropolitan Branch Trail (NCPPP, 2011a).

The private funds were forwarded on the basis of the new Metro station being an investment that would reap benefits for the businesses in the area; that is, the value of property and land would go up and more people would move into the area, adding to the customer base of the businesses. This technique is known as a special assessment district and is another example of value capture. Under such an initiative a fee is levied over a certain area for an identified new transportation project to fund the infrastructure in part or in whole. However, a crucial factor involves getting the agreement of the community to raise local taxes. Such an initiative is used instead of a TIF (see Chapters Two and Three) when the piece of infrastructure is important to the community but the future revenue stream is uncertain (Levinson and Istrate, 2011).

At the time of writing there were attempts to broker a similar deal for a Metro station between Reagan Airport and Braddock Road in Alexandria (located approximately eight miles south of Washington). This would be called Alexandria Potomac Yard and would fill one of the longest gaps that currently exist on the Metro system. Local businesses were again being encouraged to agree to the creation of a special assessment district to finance the project on the basis that such an investment would reap strong returns. However, some of these businesses felt there was no need to contribute to the project as they were under no legal obligation to do so. According to TA1, timing is very important for the public-sector purchaser and it needs to ascertain when to gain the maximum leverage on those that are most likely to gain. This might be when the decision of whether to go ahead with the new station is in the balance.

The Washington Metropolitan Area Transit Authority (WMATA) is seen as one of the most innovative authorities when it comes to using value capture (Lari et al., 2009). As well as special assessment districts they have used two other techniques to fund infrastructure. For example, the Bethesda Metro Centre, located just above the area's Metro station, used a combination of joint development and air rights to bring in extra revenue to fund future projects. The Metro Centre is a large-scale, mixed-use (i.e., office, hotel and retail) project that brings in $1.6 million in annual leasing revenues for WMATA. A joint development is a development adjacent to (or on top of) a piece of infrastructure that serves it, such as a transit station or a highway interchange. Under the Bethesda Metro Centre and other joint development arrangements, WMATA has: leased and sold its property on or adjacent to transit infrastructure; leased or sold development rights associated with its property; shared operations costs of ventilation and heating systems at transit stations; and instituted 'connections fees' for retailers who want to connect their retail space to transit stations. Payments come from the private sector for property and development rights in several forms, including one-time, lump sum payments for the purchase of property or development rights, annual lease payments, financial contributions to station construction costs and connections fees from retailers. Air rights capture the real estate value of transportation by selling or leasing the space above (or below) transportation facilities for development. Typically this is imposed after the road, rail line or transit station is constructed so it recovers value after creation, although it could be applied simultaneously with infrastructure creation. In the latter case, however, it would be a form of joint development (Levinson and Istrate, 2011). As well as the Bethesda Metro Centre, WMATA has also used air rights to help finance the Ballston Metro station in Arlington County.

URBAN REGENERATION

The following two cases come under the umbrella of what is referred to as transit-oriented development, although in the case of the Baltimore Inner Harbor this may be stretching the definition a little too far. Notwithstanding, both are examples of PPPs in which public land and buildings are used for a combination of public and private uses. Such partnerships can positively influence the local property market either by making specific areas more attractive to additional private-sector investment or by increasing the overall efficiency of government-owned assets. In both cases a public entity (a station and a harbour) were redeveloped so that the private partner could further develop the surrounding area in order to increase the land value and thereby create additional economic value and corresponding tax revenues. The overall aim of such PPPs is to leverage underutilised and underperforming public assets to create value for both private and public partners.

One of the interviewees (PA1) believes such projects have two other benefits. Firstly, they can connect what is a derelict and underused piece of public property with the more thriving and populated city centres, thus eliminating the neglected land and properties that blight cities and large towns and which can indicate an area in decline. Secondly, they can make better use of resources. This refers more specifically to sports stadia, which are generally used only at weekends or in the evenings. This interviewee believes that these should be located nearer city centres or surrounding office parks, so that parking places normally used by office workers during the day could be used by spectators when games are taking place, thereby increasing their usage. What is more, the location of sports stadia close to a city centre brings extra revenue to these cities via sales of food and other products. This interviewee believes that governments own land and have the capability of raising finance and therefore they should consider urban regeneration projects that bring a return for the private sector and also lead to greater employment, which has a number of public benefits. In most cases the governments are not selling land but leasing it, and thus the fact that they sell it at what seems like a very low value is not really relevant. Furthermore, although money lent to certain projects may be wasted in some cases, in the longer term such projects do tend to rejuvenate areas. Therefore selling land fairly cheaply has two benefits: if the project fails it proves that it is possible that there is nothing to be gained from redeveloping the area, but the government has lost very little by allowing a private developer to speculate; and in the cases in which the government has financed the project, costs are kept low by keeping the value of the land to a minimum. Thus a small investment by the public sector could breathe new life into a city.

There are various ways that private developers can rejuvenate urban areas that are in decline. These include the building of casinos, sports stadia or retail complexes, or a 'village' that combines all three—for example, the St Louis Cardinals' Village, Dallas's Victory Park and Patriots Place in Foxborough, Massachusetts. Other methods include the conversion of former DoD land and buildings into office or residential areas, or, in the case of Hunters Point Shipyard and Candlestick Point in San Francisco, a technology hub. Other disused public facilities, such as a power plant in Chester, Pennsylvania, have been converted into office space. Thus revenue generators such as tourism and entertainment replace lost industries and capital infrastructure is used for both private financial and public economic returns. The two case studies that follow are often cited as model examples of urban regeneration and are seen as highly successful PPPs.

Union Station—Washington, DC

Union Station opened in 1907 and at the time was the largest station in the world; yet by the late 1970s it had deteriorated to the extent that it was virtually uninhabitable and was in danger of demolition. However, a mixture of public and political demand led to major renovation work, via a PPP beginning in 1984, and the station now has good mix of a classical (Beaux Arts) exterior and a modern, clean interior, which, as well as the normal functions one would associate with a station, has a large number of high-end and high street shops, restaurants and fast food outlets over three floors. Additionally there is a multi-storey parking area for 1,500 vehicles, an area capable of handling 80 buses, a nine-screen cinema and ample office space. This PPP has been so successful that the station now has over 25 million visitors each year and has therefore become a major tourist attraction. The $160 million project was financed by a combination of public and private money in the following way (NCPPP, 2011b):

- Amtrak contributed $70 million for the construction of new ticketing and passenger facilities;
- DC contributed $40 million in interstate highway funds for the construction of a parking deck. These funds guaranteed a bond, whose debt service was to be paid by parking garage fees; and
- The private-sector partners provided the remaining $50 million through equity financing, serviced by revenues from commerce, rental and sales.

The PPP also involved negotiations between twelve state and federal agencies that were all affected by the project and thus shows that the problems of different laws in different jurisdictions, as raised by interviewees C1 and TA1, can be overcome.

It is generally believed that Americans are very attached to their cars and consider public transport a second-rate form of transportation that only people from lower socio-economic backgrounds use. This was not the experience of the author. The Amtrak trains that depart from Union Station to various destinations in the USA (e.g., New York, Boston, Chicago and Orlando) were normally operating at full capacity and were used by people of all backgrounds and income levels. However, as one interviewee (PA1) pointed out this has to be put into perspective. The trains running along what is referred to as the Northeast Corridor link major conurbations such as Washington, Philadelphia, New York and Boston. The actual numbers using these trains are still very small when compared to those preferring to use their cars to travel between these large cities. Moreover, another interviewee (C1) stated that there had to be strong economic connections between cities (as opposed to them simply being located close to one another) in order for high-speed passenger rail to be cost-effective, and a good way of testing for this is to study aviation data for travel between cities. This interviewee also stated that away from the Northeast Corridor the tracks are not owned by Amtrak but by freight companies, and thus organisations offering passenger services do not have the flexibility to put on more trains as freight takes priority.

It is not only the station that has benefitted from the renovation, but the surrounding area has also become what is often referred to as gentrified— that is, it has become a far more desirable area in which to live, work and socialise. In typical US fashion this area, which extends from the north of Massachusetts Avenue in Washington, DC, has been rebranded as NoMa. This is similar to the SoHo (South of Houston Street) and TriBeCa (Triangle below Canal Street) areas in New York. This gentrification has occurred due to private companies investing $3 billion in the area over the past six years (i.e., since 2005). Over that period almost 16 million square feet of the area has been developed, and from 2010 to 2011, 1,400 residents made the NoMa district their home. Companies such as Hilton Hotels and the grocer Harris Teeter, which now has a 50,000-square-foot store in the area, have moved in and a number of luxury apartment blocks have been built.

All this came about due to the Washington, DC Council creating a group known as the NoMa BID, which was tasked with co-ordinating public and private investment, providing cleaning and safety services, and generally promoting the area. It is clear that they have been very successful in completing these tasks. A further contributing factor came about due to another PPP, which spent $110 million developing the New York Avenue Metro station, thereby linking the area to a public transportation system (see the foregoing Dulles Metrorail case study for more on this). NoMa still suffers from an east side/west side divide, with the former not much transformed from the days when the area was seen as a no-man's land, populated mostly by warehouses. However, the BID hopes to soften this divide by working with Amtrak to repair, repaint and light the connecting underpasses, which have created a physical barrier. Notwithstanding, there are plans to continue developing the area as a whole with proposals for a gym, a child-care facility, more bars, a park and even the resurrection of the Uline Arena (where the Beatles once played and Malcolm X spoke) as a concert hall or movie theatre. Moreover, residential units continue to be built and a further 2,000 people could eventually move into the area.

The gentrification of an area is not always a boon for all citizens. If someone is a property owner then he or she can benefit from the higher property values that urban redevelopment often brings. However, if he or she is a tenant then rent increases can force them out of the area and communities break down. This has been the experience in the U Street area of Washington, DC, where the Afro-American community has been disrupted due to rising property values. Moreover, Union Station has almost become a victim of its own success. According to TA1, Amtrak could operate at 30% extra capacity, which means it is currently looking to expand to maximise customer revenue. At the same time, due to the increase in rail passengers, the Metro station that serves Union Station also has capacity issues and thus it too is looking to expand. However, such expansions are likely to encroach on one another's areas as well as that of the retail and food outlets.

Inner Harbor Area—Baltimore

The inner harbour area of Baltimore is an inspiring site. The harbour has an outlet into the Patapsco River and then eventually into the Chesapeake Bay, and developers have made maximum use of the remaining three sides of the harbour, which have been fully pedestrianised. What was once a rundown area of the city now has a wide variety of tourist attractions (including the Maryland Science Centre, National Aquarium, American Visionary Art Museum and Port Discovery Children's Museum), three shopping centres (with the normal variety of retail outlets, cafes and restaurants), hotels, office blocks and high-rise residential accommodation. The developers have also made the most of the nautical association with numerous forms of water transport and permanent exhibitions, including the USS Constellation (a ship used in the American Civil War), the US Submarine Torsk, the US Coast Guard Cutter Taney and the Lightship 116, Chesapeake. Additionally there is a viewing gallery on the 27th floor of Baltimore's World Trade Center and a modern visitor's centre. The whole vista is further enhanced by an impressive array of personal boats and yachts on one side of the harbour. This development took place between the 1970s and 1980s following a long period of economic decline.

Having once been one of the leading US industrial and port cities, during the 1950s Baltimore suffered from large job losses in the manufacturing sector and suburbanisation, which both contributed to a falling population (Levine, 2000). However, under the leadership of Mayor William Donald Schaefer (1971–1986) a renaissance strategy was devised, the focal point of which was the city's inner harbour, which was at the time a wasteland comprising rundown warehouses and decaying wharves. The funding for this urban regeneration came mainly from the public purse and private developers were offered incentives (financial and otherwise) to begin investing in the area. According to Levine (2000) this led to over $800 million of private investment being leveraged between 1976 and 1986, almost half of which went into downtown projects such as the Inner Harbor. Moreover a convention centre was also built in the area, which meant extra customers for the hotels, some of which received below market-rate loans to build around the harbour. During the 1980s more than 3.5 million square feet of what is referred to as 'Class A' office space was developed and 15 hotels opened (Levine, 2000). This together with the luxury housing that was built in the area added up to $1.6 billion of development, 90% of which came from private investment. The pace of growth slowed in the 1990s as Baltimore, like many cities worldwide, found itself a victim of the end of the property market boom. However, Schaefer's successor as mayor, Kurt L. Schmoke, was not deterred and pumped more money into the area, which resulted in projects such as: the building of two sports stadiums; the expansion of the convention centre; the building of the Columbus Centre (a marine-biology facility); the provision of more subsidies for hotels; and the building of a large entertainment complex known as the Power Plant.

There are many benefits of such an area to any city, including: employment in the shops, restaurants, hotels and tourist attractions; increased revenue from tourists attracted to the area; higher property values; higher rental values; lower vacancy rates; better rates of absorption (i.e., the ability of the real estate market to absorb or sell all of the properties for sale in a given amount of time); higher densities; and increased tax revenues. Moreover, the location of multi-purpose sports stadiums in the vicinity can bring about some of the advantages outlined by interviewee PA1 earlier. At the time of writing there was to be a further enhancement to the harbour area, which is also the main port of Baltimore. This is also via a PPP and consists of new 50-foot berths, which, according to officials from the Maryland Department of Transportation (2011), will be built in time for the extension to the Panama Canal. This operating-berth depth of 50 feet is required for the type of mega-ships that will soon be able to travel to Maryland via the Panama Canal. When this work is completed in mid-2012, Baltimore will be one of two ports on the US east coast with this depth of operating-berth. It is apparently one of the largest PPP projects in the northeast of the country and will result in extra revenues and lower capital expenditure for the state of Maryland.

One further advantage of both these and other urban regeneration projects according to TA1 is that they result in the non-fragmentation of a region. In other words cities are no longer seen in terms of good and bad areas, but as a good place to work, live and socialise overall. This leads in particular to the attraction of young, educated people, which makes it possible for businesses to build themselves around the energy and creativity of these workers. However, whilst this has happened in the Union Station area (see previous case study), this has not been the experience of the Baltimore Inner Harbor project. Indeed, according to Levine (2000, p. 124) just 15 'blocks away from the Inner Harbor and expanding to broad patches of the urban landscape were desolate neighbourhoods marked by social exclusion, high rates of crime and drug abuse, deepening ghetto poverty, and dilapidated or abandoned housing, where much of the city's predominantly black population lived'. Therefore claims that Baltimore had become a 'renaissance city' as a result of its urban regeneration efforts were inaccurate. Moreover, the sustainability of tourism as an income generator when compared to sectors such as manufacturing and services has been questioned. Barringer (2001), when looking at 'carnival cities' (such as Baltimore) that use attractions like convention centres, casinos and sports stadiums to bring in tourist money, believes they often end up spending far more in subsidies than they gain in revenue. Moreover, Levine (2000) feels that, in the rush to attract investment, officials in Baltimore did not carry out the appropriate due diligence and thus deals were structured badly, loans were not fully repaid and taxpayers ended up paying for failed projects such as the Columbus Centre.

CONCLUSIONS

The foregoing case studies highlight contrasting projects, both in scope, degrees of completion and the amount of private finance used. The two transportation projects are attempting to deal with Washington's severe congestion problems in different ways. The I-95 HOV/HOT lanes PPP will add extra capacity and also bring in more toll revenue, whereas the Dulles Metro extension (and further additions to the network) will hopefully lead to less strain on the road system. However, the latter has faced financing difficulties, which have been partially resolved by the use of innovative value-capture techniques. Indeed, WMATA has been particularly successful in bringing in revenue via mechanisms such as special assessment districts, joint development and air rights. The two urban regeneration schemes are widely considered to be highly successful in both fostering redevelopment of an underutilised area and changing the pattern of physical and economic growth in the regions. It should be noted, however, that not all urban regeneration schemes have been successful (see Scribner [2011] for a number of examples) and gentrification can lead to certain residents becoming unable to afford to live in an area. Moreover, whereas the success of the Union Station redevelopment has spread to an area known as NoMa, this has not been the case with the Baltimore Inner Harbor PPP. In this case there are still some rundown, poverty-stricken and crime-ridden areas not that far away. The financial arrangements of this project have also been called into question.

9 Conclusions and Areas for Further Research

DIFFERENCES BETWEEN THE USA AND UK

This chapter aims to compare and contrast the use of PPPs in the USA and UK following both a review of some of the literature and the interviews and observations carried out by the author whilst in the former country. Moreover, areas for future research will be considered and the objectives outlined in Chapter One will be reflected upon.

There are clearly some major differences between the two countries that have to be considered before any discussion about PPPs can take place. Firstly the USA has a federal system of government, whereby sovereignty is constitutionally divided between a central governing authority and constituent political units, in this case states. Therefore, perhaps a fairer comparison would have been between the use of PPPs in these states and their use in the now far more constitutionally diverse countries that make up the UK. States have far more autonomy than local government in the UK and are able to make their own laws and issue their own bonds (receiving their own credit ratings).

This leads to another difference between the two countries, which is the much greater power of local government in the USA (Peters and Pierre, 1998). This contrasts with local government being seen traditionally as the poor relation to central government in the UK (Stewart, 2000). Under the Conservative administration of 1979–1997 the central-local relationship in the UK could probably be summarised by what Stewart (2000) calls the strange phenomenon of a local perception of increasing control and a central perception of a lack of control. However, despite a feeling that should Labour to return to government, as they did in 1997, there would be greater levels of freedom for local authorities, this did not eventually materialise (Wall and Martin, 2003). However, under the Local Government Act of 2003, local authorities were given greater freedom over their capital expenditures; therefore whilst most of their revenue still came from central government, it now had less say over how this money was spent. Thus some local authorities opted for what was called the Prudential Borrowing Framework (PBF), which provided an alternative to PPP. Indeed, as PBF excludes the private sector from all aspects of a project apart from construction, it is closer to traditional procurement. However, Hood et al. (2007) believe that whilst the PBF has benefits it is not as robust as PPP regarding the treatment and allocation of risk. In contrast, local government in the USA has always had much greater freedom over the way they spend any money allocated to them. Moreover, they can raise money via taxes and, as with states, can issue their own bonds to raise finance. It should also be noted that both state and local authority bonds are tax-exempt, which means that interest payments are not subject to federal income tax. In effect this means that the federal government is indirectly providing funding for any projects financed via this means.

One also has to consider a different relationship between government and the private sector in the two countries. Peters and Pierre (1998) describe the concept of governance without government in the USA, and highlight the fact that it has been described as stateless society, which immediately makes it different from European states. Moreover, government in the USA has a history of utilising the private sector (both for-profit and non-profit) to help make and implement policy (Salamon, 1981; Kettl, 1987). As a result of this there appears to be less resistance in the USA when the government divests itself of functions and permits the private sector to do what it can do better (Peters and Pierre, 1998). These authors go on to state that there are many more things that Americans consider appropriate for the private sector to do, which again sets them apart from Europeans. Notwithstanding, there are some notable differences between the two countries when it comes to the use of PPPs and these are now outlined ahead.

FINANCE

Boardman et al. (2005) highlight an important difference between the USA and UK; in the former most of the long-term infrastructure PPPs are publicly funded, but the majority in the latter are now privately funded. However, this might start to change for two main reasons. Firstly, as Brown (2007, p. 324) indicates in the USA there are 'investors with large cash holdings and long-term payout responsibilities such as pension funds and insurance companies (that) are looking for moderate returns that are stable and predictable and carry a minimum of risk', and thus infrastructure PPPs could be the ideal projects in which to invest. This availability of money via pension funds was a point made by several of the interviewees, who felt that a great deal of private money was available via the world's largest funds, which have come to view infrastructure as a separate investment category, much like a stock or a bond. It is estimated that from 2008 to 2011, 30 of the biggest investors in infrastructure channelled as much as $180 billion into these types of investments. These investors include the Australian bank Macquarie Capital, as well as some of the largest pension plans in Europe,

Australia and Canada. According to one of the interviewees (PF1) there is somewhere in the region of $95 billion being raised by various funds for infrastructure investments globally. Whilst not all of this money will be used in the USA there will still be a substantial amount available.

Why infrastructure is so appealing for these investors is the steady, predictable income that it can provide. The theory is that people need to get to work, use electricity and flush toilets, so a toll road, an electric utility or a water utility tends to deliver cash no matter what happens in the stock market on any given day. However, what also becomes clear from the interviews is that the investors have to see some sort of return. Therefore whilst there would always be a market for toll roads, PPP projects common in the UK such as the building of hospitals and schools would have little appeal. Another interviewee (PA1) believes that local private construction industry pension funds should be used to finance local infrastructure projects. He or she feels this would bring about three main benefits: a financial return for the pension fund; local jobs; and, due to a feeling of ownership by the workforce, there would be fewer stoppages and other problems caused by industrial disputes. As well as pension funds and insurance companies, potential financing could also come from global infrastructure conglomerates (e.g., Balfour Beatty, Skanska), dedicated infrastructure funds (e.g., those of Goldman Sachs, the Blackstone Group), sovereign wealth funds (e.g., Temasek Holdings, Mumtalakat Bahrain Investments) and family offices (e.g., Ambani Family, Cascade).

The second reason there is likely to be more private investment in the future is due to the dire state of the US economy. There has traditionally been more private investment in US roads; for example, out of the total cost of $1.8 billion for the Florida I-595 PPP, $208 million came from private equity (Desilets, 2009). Papajohn et al. (2011) also found a number of states using the DBFO model for transport PPPs and that finance was a major reason for going down this route. However, according to Papajohn et al. (2011) the majority of the financial instruments available for funding transportation PPPs are not issued by private organisations. Nevertheless, there was at the time of writing increasing pressure on state budgets and less money available from central government to assist with much-needed infrastructure projects, particularly in transportation. The author was slightly surprised to find a number of books and articles advocating PFI types of deals whereby the private sector provides project finance (see, for example, DiNapoli, 2011; Engel et al., 2011; Geddes, 2011). Whilst these articles come with a number of caveats and suggestions of best practice, some of the many failures of UK PFI projects are not fully analysed. Moreover, several of the interviewees either advocate the use of more private money or acknowledge that it is likely to become more commonplace. Therefore, just as the UK is taking a far more cautious approach to PPPs because of problems inherited from the former administration, the USA seems to be embracing its most used model (e.g. PFI) in the former country.

There are, however, some alternative finance arrangements currently being used in the USA, with one of the most interesting being the concession or long-term lease agreement. These are used for what are known as brownfield, or existing, PPPs as opposed to greenfield, or new builds. They are used in the transportation sector and on roads that are already being tolled by the state authority. Under a concession agreement a private partner will take over the maintenance and operation of a facility, along with any necessary improvements or expansion, for a large upfront fee. The private partner aims to recoup this fee through its right to the toll revenue, which it will hope to maximise through better availability (e.g., accidents and debris cleared quickly, better drainage), cost savings (e.g., electronic tolling) and, more controversially, the increasing of tolls either generally or at peak traffic times. Under such a PPP the public authority retains ownership and would appear to have abdicated all risk to the private partner. Moreover, if the concession fee is large enough the state or local authority will have sufficient funds to pay off any debts and still have a surplus to be used for future investments. Although there have been a number of these, two of the best known are the Chicago Skyway project and the Indiana Toll Road, both of which have been referred to already in this book.

There are obvious barriers for trying to market a similar scheme in the UK, with the main one being the lack of existing toll roads in the country. Road pricing is often put forward as a way of reducing the amount of traffic on the roads as well as bringing in much needed finance, but meets fierce resistance by drivers and their lobby groups. Any toll roads in the UK are normally privately operated, with the private sector recouping costs to cover upfront construction and ongoing operating costs. However, there is potentially a market there, with a number of large international firms seemingly keen to invest in such projects. Having said that, such investors will be keeping a close eye on the Chicago and Indiana deals, both of which are struggling to make sufficient revenue to keep up with debt repayments. Whilst the amount of traffic using both highways might increase if the economy starts to improve, it may be too late if in the interim the private partners have gone bankrupt (Holeywell, 2011).

A far more controversial concession type of PPP also took place in Chicago, and this was the selling of the city's parking meters for a 75-year term to a private company in 2008. Whilst this was initially seen as a good deal for the city, there has been a lot more criticism recently (see, for example, Preston, 2010) that states that taxpayers are going to lose out in the long term. However, according to one of the interviewees (PI2) many of the problems do not rest with the PPP itself. For example, the city's officials spent a lot of the large payment on short-term, politically motivated projects and did not consider saving money for the future. Moreover, a recent audit that declared that present value of the future revenue to be too high was poorly executed and used the wrong discount figures. Also, the company that won the concession modernised the city's parking meters and raised the prices in some locations, which was clearly going to be unpopular. The interviewee believes, however, that it priced parking in popular areas properly, which the city had never done previously, and thus this led to a more efficient allocation of resources. This is a similar argument to that made by Geddes (2011) about the pricing of toll roads, which he feels makes users more aware of the resource they are using.

The USA has also used a number of techniques that come under the umbrella of value capture. In Chapters Two, Four and Eight references have been made to mechanisms such as TIF, joint development, special assessment districts and air rights, but three others have also been used in the USA, albeit not widely. These are as follows (Levinson and Istrate, 2011).

- *Impact fees*

  This is a one-off fee levied on a developer who is looking to build homes or offices in a particular area. The fee is levied on each building constructed by a developer. This technique works on the principle that government provides infrastructure and land development consumes it. Such fees work better when there are many developers, none of whom alone would have the scale to do a joint development, and in the context of roads where there is a dispersed origin and destination pattern.

- *Land-value taxes*

  Under such a scheme the property tax (a major source of funding transportation projects in the USA) is reformed by separating the value of a property associated with land from that associated with the building. Because the value of the land is determined by its accessibility, which is created by the community at large via transportation networks and the location of activities, a tax only on land value better captures the benefits of transportation than a tax on both land and buildings. The nature of the land-value tax makes it difficult to use it to fund a single project, and it is therefore more appropriate as a source for funding a comprehensive transportation programme. Hawaii and Pennsylvania (particularly Pittsburgh) have used the land-value tax, but otherwise it is not used widely across the USA.

- *Transportation utility fees*

  These fees replace the share of general fund tax revenue going to transportation with a charge that is roughly proportional to expected transportation use. Therefore, these fees tie the benefits to costs of infrastructure and are much simpler to implement than a more comprehensive user fee. Such a technique has been used in a number of states, including Colorado, Florida, Idaho, Oregon, Texas, Washington and Wisconsin. These fees are levied annually on properties within an area likely to benefit from transportation infrastructure and earmark transportation funding, separating it from general revenue. This financing mechanism increases the tax base over which transportation charges can be levied more than property taxes, because non-taxable properties still must pay a utility fee.

There are also a number of financing schemes in the USA that are based on taxation. For example, DC used payment in lieu of taxes (PILOT) to fund the Oyster School/Henry Adams House referred to in Chapter Five. Under this arrangement a private developer financed, designed and built the school and also constructed a $29-million, nine-story, 211-unit apartment building on the excess land of the site. The school was financed by a 35-year tax-exempt bond issued by DC, which is being paid off via PILOT by the owner of the apartment building. Therefore, the new school was constructed without incurring any public expenditure. Unlike TIF, whereby payments are made from the growth in a district's property values, as its name suggests, no taxes are paid under PILOT. Therefore, the effect on the area's overall tax revenue is more difficult to determine. There are many examples all over the world whereby organisations are offered a variety of tax relief schemes should they locate in a certain area, and perhaps therefore PILOT is closer to those schemes than value capture. Arguments may be made that, although such developments take place without incurring any public expenditure and the public may gain from the general improvement of an area, they still lose out when businesses are exempt from paying taxation.

Another method via which PPPs can be financed is sales tax. This was used as a method of funding improvement to the Verizon Center, a sports and entertainment complex in Washington, DC where both basketball and ice hockey are played. In order to pay for $50 million of improvements, the DC government authorised an increase in sales tax on Verizon Center tickets and merchandise from 5.75% to 10%. The original centre, which opened in 1997, and its surrounding infrastructure had been financed via a number of private and public sources, including the issue of $43 million of Arena Revenue Bonds. These are to be paid back via the imposition of an arena tax on the surrounding business community, including hotels, car rental companies, bars and restaurants, which are likely to benefit from the new arena. DC also used a ballpark tax to partly fund the building of the new Washington Nationals Baseball stadium, Nationals Park, which opened in 2008 in the southeast of the city. Once again this tax is imposed on local businesses, which then pass on the cost to their customers. The Washington deals mentioned here were all negotiated by either the Downtown DC BID or the Capitol Riverfront BID. Interestingly A4 pointed out that a lot of the organisations located around the Nationals Park arena are federal agencies, which must have limited the amount of money raised via the ballpark tax.

It may seem strange that, whilst nobody likes paying extra taxes, businesses agree to pay extra rates or don't put up more resistance when their burden is increased due to developments in their location. However, as highlighted by A4, there is an acknowledgement by these private companies that the public sector has made a considerable contribution to such projects, either directly by funding or indirectly by selling land at below market rates. Another interviewee, A5, stated that developers tend to make money whatever the situation. In some cases they will sell the buildings fairly quickly and therefore avoid paying the property tax on the increased value. Furthermore, private companies often gain when there is greater density. This interviewee also highlighted the importance of established guidelines and rules when dealing with developers. Such people do not like uncertainty in a project as they will find it difficult to obtain funding themselves.

PPPS IN AN ECONOMIC RECESSION

It is perhaps noteworthy that the DBFO types of PPPs are being proposed in the USA as a response to the economic downturn and a much-needed upgrade of the nation's infrastructure, particularly its roads. In many ways PFI came about due to the macroeconomic dislocation of the 1970s and 1980s, which had led to the UK's infrastructure being neglected as public spending was directed to what were seen as more pressing needs. PPPs in which the private sector provides the finance do seem like an optimal solution to such a predicament. Jobs are created, the infrastructure improves (leading to further economic development) and the large upfront costs are borne by the private sector. However, as stated previously the state officials need to be fully aware of the problems associated with this model as the focus changes from leveraging the skills and know-how of the private sector to also needing its capital. Notwithstanding, there were some uses of PPPs to boost economic growth that could perhaps be given greater consideration in the UK.

Employment schemes referred to in Chapter Seven such as One City, One Hire and Hire One Atlanta are programmes that appear to utilise private capacity and public money (tax breaks, wage subsidies and funding for training) to the benefit of the unemployed. However, other so-called job-creation PPPs have been seen as little more than political cronyism. For example, Texas governor and former potential Republican candidate for the 2012 presidential election, Rick Perry, was accused of wasting state money when $4.5 million was invested in Convergen LifeSciences Inc. to develop a cancer-fighting drug using nanotechnology. The money came from a job-creation fund meant to spur innovation and research at universities and in the private sector. It was controversial as the company put in only $1,000 dollars of its own money and one of the company's founders, David Nance, was not only a Perry contributor but also had been the founder and CEO of another biotechnology company that had gone bankrupt in 2008. As Rubin (2011) commented at the time, taken to the national level this sort of public-private cooperation inevitably leads to giant bureaucracies, politicisation of business decisions and a playing field tipped heavily in favour of those big and rich enough to gain political access.

There have been less controversial PPPs that have the aim of boosting employment and economic growth, which come under the umbrella of R&D. Such PPPs normally involve a government department funding projects that bring together universities and businesses. A number of these were announced between September 2010 and September 2011, covering areas such as biofuels, cybersecurity, business start-ups for university scientists and engineers, the improvement of science, technology, engineering and math education, weather research and the establishment of an electrical power integrated systems' R&D centre. Such projects have a particular poignancy during an economic downturn as a mixture of public and private money and expertise is used to create new business ventures and therefore jobs.

A final way that PPPs can be used during a recession is through economic development or urban regeneration programmes. Areas are revitalised by overhauling their infrastructures in order to boost revenues by attracting businesses, residents, shoppers and possibly tourists. Such PPPs are often referred to as leveraging public-sector assets, such as land and property, in order to maximise their value. There are some obvious ways the government can do this, such as selling off land no longer needed by the DoD. Such sales not only bring in much needed revenue but also, by reducing the government's real estate, lower its costs. However, when states or local authorities form partnerships with private developers in order to redevelop urban areas, there can be mixed results. Whilst the Union Station and Baltimore Inner Harbor projects are considered to be a success, Scribner (2011, p. 23) feels that the US 'government's recent expanded role in real estate development has increased taxpayer exposure to risk, socialized costs, and concentrated the benefits into the hands of select private developers and special interests'. Moreover, as seen in Chapter Eight the success of the Inner Harbor PPP did not spread to nearby areas of Baltimore, which remain deprived.

RISK TRANSFER AND VALUE FOR MONEY

These two factors have dominated the debate about PPPs in the UK for many years, with numerous writers claiming that the taxpayer does not get VFM from a PPP arrangement and that risk is often transferred to the private sector in name only (see Chapter Two). However, from the comments in Chapter Seven it is evident that, although both are seen as important factors in determining project success, they are not dominant issues. This backs up the comment of Papajohn et al. (2011) that 'even states that are leaders in PPPs, such as Texas and Virginia, have not fully realized the potential of PPPs because risks, risk sharing, and the complexity of funding is not fully understood'. Moreover, Morallos et al. (2009) found very few agencies using VFM analysis tools in their study of US transportation PPPs. Financial risk was considered to be the most overriding concern, and even what other nations would call demand risk was framed in purely financial terms—for example, would the toll revenue be sufficient to enable the contractor to service the debt? Furthermore, where PPPs had failed there was little evidence that these were bailed out by the public sector with the costs of failure subsequently borne by the taxpayer. The example of San Diego's South Bay Expressway, which led to losses for equity holders and the opportunity for repurchase by the state at a much lower cost, clearly shows that the private sector alone was exposed to financial risk. With regard to VFM, whilst a full cost-benefit analysis is encouraged, the USA seems to be again looking towards a UK model, the PSC. As with PFI in general there has been a lot of criticism about this model, and perhaps a greater analysis of some of its shortcomings is required before it becomes widely used. However, it is encouraging to see that one state has modified its PSC, thereby circumventing some of these shortcomings.

PUBLIC-SECTOR EXPERTISE

One of the surprising findings in Chapter Seven was that, whilst it was acknowledged that there is a lack of public expertise in areas such as contract negotiation and monitoring, there seem to be fewer problems with the contracts themselves. Although there was some acknowledgement that contracts could be too rigid and budgets less flexible under PPPs, many interviewees believe that good working relationships existed between the partners and that the correct incentives and KPIs led to a superior performance by the private sector. Nevertheless, the USA is looking at the dedicated PPP units of a number of countries, including the UK, as a means of building expertise. In the UK this role is currently carried out by Infrastructure UK, which is an HMT unit. However, the establishment of such a unit is not enough in itself to prevent poor PPP deals going through, as sometimes happened when Infrastructure UK's predecessor, Partnerships UK, fulfilled this role.

One recommendation made by Vining and Boardman (2008) as to how PPPs in general could be better administered is to separate the various agencies that analyse, evaluate, administer and monitor PPPs, the supposition being that it is quite hard for an agency that has selected a particular private partner for a project to then objectively monitor them. This is seen as less of a problem in the USA due to a separation of powers; therefore governments find it easier to generate separate oversight agencies and avoid conflicts of interest that may arise due to the same agency carrying out too many important roles. However, Engel et al. (2011) believe the USA is not immune to such problems and recommend that the internal structure of any public agency involved in a PPP be split appropriately. It was interesting that with regard to contract negotiation and management, the findings from the interviews appear to contradict some of the literature, particularly in the area of urban regeneration. Clearly only a very small number of people took part in the interviews, but possibly lessons have been learnt and the public sector in the USA is getting more professional in its handling of PPPs.

PUBLIC OPPOSITION

One difference highlighted in the case studies, two of the interviews (A1 and A5) and also briefly in Chapters Three, Four and Five is a greater participation of US citizens in matters that have an impact on their locales. Whilst there are very active local interest groups in the UK, it is difficult to imagine a PPP not being awarded to a certain contractor due to local opposition, as happened with Texas State Highway 121 (Battaglio and Khankarli, 2008) or Minnesota Trunk Highway 212 (Istrate and Puentes, 2011). Indeed the FHwA (2005b) considers public opposition one of the main barriers to the use of PPPs in transportation projects (see Chapter Four). Moreover, Morallos et al. (2009) note that agency officials in the USA found that the lack of public support can be a hindrance to transportation PPPs. Whereas the prospect of any tolled road tends to face significant opposition due to equity issues and the perception that the highway systems should be free, PPPs face additional challenges resulting from a public distrust of private corporations. The fear that any private entity will end up increasing any toll fees can make it more difficult for such PPPs to garner support. It is interesting to note that in some areas there is a distrust of private organisations; however, there is undoubtedly a greater mistrust of government in the USA.

Morallos et al. (2009, p. 34) also note that 'public support also influences political support, because elected officials will most likely respond in a manner akin to their jurisdiction'. One interviewee (C1) also agrees with this point, stating that 'elected officials have very receptive antennae when it comes to unhappy voters'. The author has been at public meetings where the prospect of schools becoming PPPs has been discussed, and, whilst a large number of concerns were raised by parents and other stakeholders, there was still a feeling that the project was being presented as a fait accompli. Notwithstanding, one of the interviewees (A2) believes that in some cases what appeared to be the actions of members of a community was actually being motivated by the interests of powerful lobby groups who were opposed to a particular project. Therefore such opposition may not be as spontaneous and ingenuous as it seems. An example of such a group according to A5 is the large public-sector employee unions, whose members tend to lose their jobs when more efficient private companies take over the running of roads and other infrastructure. Politicians firstly don't like taking on these unions and secondly don't like to be accused of cutting public jobs.

However, such workers are not incentivised to do things any differently and thus public roads and other assets are not run as efficiently as they could be.

SOCIAL INFRASTRUCTURE

In the USA PPPs have not been much used for the building of schools and hospitals, which is in contrast to the experience of the UK. However, interviewee A4 believes there may come a time when private-sector health providers become interested in managing facilities, and thus DBOM deals in the health sector may begin to emerge. Moreover, A5 believes there is no reason why the private sector should not get more involved with the building and maintenance of schools, leaving the public sector to their own area of expertise—teaching. Once again the interviewee believes opposition from public-sector employees, who all have a vote and could lose their jobs, would be a major stumbling block.

This leads to an argument that was made by a large number of interviewees—why should the public sector own any capital assets? The whole purpose of such assets is to generate revenue, and yet the public sector rarely does this. As seen with some of the transportation and urban regeneration PPPs, the private sector can leverage more money out of land and other assets and therefore should have more opportunity to do this. Moreover, as seen earlier and in some of the examples put forward in Chapter Seven, the public-sector employees who control these assets are not incentivised to think creatively or run them more efficiently and thus the taxpayer loses out. There are clearly many arguments against such a viewpoint, but it was interesting how many times it was made.

THE CATEGORISATION OF PPPS

There is no doubt that the definition of PPPs is far wider in the USA than it is in the UK. As stated in Chapter One, private can refer to both for-profit and not-for-profit organisations (although the distinction may not actually be that great) and even private individuals. They also include arrangements which would be categorised in the UK as outsourcing or contracting out. In some cases simple supply arrangements have also come under the umbrella of PPPs. An example of this is when public-sector organisations use commercial software to help them become more efficient or effective. Surely because the public sector do not produce such items themselves and due to modern collaborative supplier arrangements, where there is greater interaction with the customer, this is just a normal commercial arrangement? Taken to an extreme, it could be stated that the use of vending machines selling soft drinks and chocolate bars in public-sector organisations is a PPP. Another arrangement with a software organisation is harder to categorise.

In 2010 a number of states, including Oregon, Minnesota, Delaware and Tennessee, announced partnerships with Microsoft. The aim of these partnerships was for Microsoft to provide free online technology training to workers, the unemployed and any other individuals looking for opportunities to improve their computer skills. The public benefit is clear, but it could be argued that this is a true PPP only if Microsoft is looking for some return from this programme, known as Elevate America. In other examples used in this book, brand awareness (although this hardly seems necessary for Microsoft in the USA) and other forms of marketing might be considered an appropriate return. Moreover, it could be that Microsoft hope that such actions will lead to future sales of its many products and services to both states and individuals across the USA. However, there is perhaps a fine line between this sort of arrangement and corporate social responsibility.

There is a tendency in the USA to class much clearer examples of corporate social responsibility as PPPs. A nationwide scheme that was started in 2010 called the No Kid Hungry campaign had the laudable aim of ending childhood hunger in the USA by 2015, by increasing access to nutrition education and to federal programmes whereby free meals or food is provided to children from certain backgrounds. The private participation in such a scheme consisted of media outlets promoting the scheme and a number of retailers linking themselves to the aforementioned federal programmes. This scheme was labelled as a PPP, but regardless of the motives behind the private companies involved such a categorisation stretches the definition too broadly. Likewise, some health schemes in the USA that involve the government providing funding and private providers (both doctors and dentists) working either pro bono or at a reduced fee to help poor families are in the author's opinion also wrongly categorised as PPPs (see the example of CMOHI in Chapter Five). Moreover, initiatives to reduce childhood obesity by government working with foods manufacturers to expand lower-calorie options, change product recipes to lower the calorie content, or reducing portion sizes of single-serve products are classed as PPPs in the USA but wouldn't be in the UK. Finally schemes that are really just the government providing grants to businesses to improve their productivity are also called PPPs. In the case of an initiative announced in March 2011 whereby small and medium businesses in the US Midwest were to be given money to enhance their technological capabilities, the partnership came from the government and larger private companies providing the funding. However, the end result will not be any form of public service delivery, except possibly employment, so again it is felt the term is being used incorrectly.

It could be stated that no product or service is provided purely by the public or private sector. For example, the private sector relies on infrastructure, such as toll-free roads, and an educated workforce, which are both mainly provided by the public sector. Likewise in order to function, all public-sector organisations need products and services that are provided by private-sector companies. Clearly not everything produced or provided by both sectors can be categorised as a PPP, but from the literature and interviews it is clear that in the USA the boundaries are being stretched and the term is becoming overused.

AREAS FOR FURTHER RESEARCH

Some of the limitations of this study were highlighted in Chapter Seven. These are the fairly limited geographical coverage and the small number of sectors examined in any great detail. Therefore, any future comparison of the two countries could widen the scope of this study. Moreover, as mentioned in Chapter Seven, perhaps given the autonomy of states when it comes to decision-making and the growing independence of Northern Ireland, Scotland and Wales, a more accurate comparison may be conducted by comparing the use of PPPs in a state with one of the four countries that make up the UK.

The book was predicated on the categorising of PPPs in the UK under the DFBO model. This was mainly due to the fact that it is this approach that has created the most debate in the academic community. However, there are many different types of PPP in the UK and future research may compare these with their US equivalents. Indeed, whilst the Coalition Government has shown some opposition to infrastructure PPPs, its quest to reduce the size of government may lead to an increased role for the private sector in public service delivery, and therefore in future there may be a focus on different partnership arrangements. Moreover, the literature review disregarded US PPPs that did not fit the author's definition. Therefore a number of what may have been highly innovative and effective arrangements, which the UK could possibly learn from, were not considered. A future study could therefore widen the coverage regarding different types of partnerships.

Finally, as this book was being written there was a groundswell of opinion in the USA that one approach to get the economy moving again, particularly in the transportation sector, is to use the PFI type of PPP. It would perhaps be interesting to see if this model is increasingly utilised and, if so, if some of the problems encountered in the UK are avoided.

CONCLUDING COMMENTS

This book set out to answer the following questions:

- How has the PPP process evolved in the USA?
- Are there major differences when it comes to the use of PPPs between different states?

- Is the private sector viewed with less suspicion in the USA when it comes to projects that would normally fall under the aegis of the public sector?
- If so, is this due to different political systems, with the neo-liberal, free market thinking still more in favour in the USA?
- Are public-sector employees in the USA better when it comes to negotiation with private-sector partners?
- How do key players in the PPP process in the USA: define project success; determine the merits and drawbacks of the initiative; and deal with controversial elements of the scheme in the UK such as value for money and risk transfer?
- Are there any areas of good practice or lessons that can be learnt for the future development of PPPs in the UK?

The first question can really be answered by stating that the USA has a long history of PPPs. Indeed, it is the public sector that is the relative new arrival to service provision in many areas. However, more recently it appears that it is looking to models such as PFI to evolve the process further. Whilst this is perhaps understandable due to the state of the US economy at the time of writing, it is not evident that enough analysis has been conducted on the many problems this model has created in the UK. With regard to the second question, the literature review and Chapters Seven and Eight have hopefully made it clear that there are major differences between different states with regard to the use of PPPs.

The answer to the third question is undoubtedly yes. There is little faith in the US government in general, and although in most nations the private sector is always viewed as more efficient, effective and economic, it is held in much higher regard in the USA. Profit making on the back of public service delivery is not seen as unethical in most areas and, in answer to question four, this is probably down to a more meritocratic culture. Nonetheless, the public has in the past blocked transportation PPPs from progressing due to a fear of toll rises; thus there is not total trust in the private sector. Additionally there is a mistrust of foreign ownership of infrastructure assets and a growing opposition to returns via assets, such as roads, leaving the country.

The answer to the fifth question is probably no. Indeed, think tanks in the USA are encouraging policymakers to look to countries like the UK, Australia and Canada, which have set up dedicated PPP units. Despite the long history of PPPs in the USA, centrally based support, legislation or guidance seems relatively new. However, most interviewees believe that despite this lack of expertise the private sector generally performs well due to incentives and KPIs.

Hopefully the answer to the sixth question was supplied in Chapter Seven and also in the foregoing subsection on risk and value for money. A lot of the interviewees' comments are probably no different to what would have been said in any survey regarding the use of PPPs in other countries.

However, some notable differences are that factors such as improved public-sector staff morale and fewer administrative duties for senior personnel are not seen as important in ensuring project success, although this could be down to the relatively low number of assets being created via PPPs. Likewise, common drawbacks with the scheme in the UK such as contract rigidity, less flexibility in budgets, a long tender process and lack of transparency are not seen as major factors. Finally, despite some dissenting voices, it is clear that PPPs are more acceptable in the USA.

With regard to the final question, there are perhaps a number of areas of good practice and lessons that could be learnt by the UK, and these include:

- Test the market for concession or long-term agreements and those where the private-sector return is limited to marketing or, more specifically, brand awareness. As well as being used in the case of the large transit authority mentioned in Chapter Seven, a similar arrangement was used for the bike sharing scheme in Paris. Here the cost of the infrastructure was paid for by the advertising company JCDecaux, who in return expected the rights to advertise on every bike used in the scheme and any associated property. In such contracts all risk is with the private contractor. In Washington, DC an advertising company, Clear Channel, entered a 20-year deal with the city to renovate all its bus shelters in return for exclusive advertising rights. However, a combination of the economic recession and the rise of promotion via the internet has resulted in a reduction in the number of companies looking to use outdoor advertising. Therefore the city still has its new bus shelters but Clear Channel has experienced falling revenues from the PPP;

- Look into some of the value capture and taxation techniques currently in use in the USA. In Chapter Two it was noted that TIF is already being used in Scotland, so perhaps this and other applications could also be used throughout the UK; BIDs are common throughout the UK, but they would not use the range of arrangements referred to earlier in this chapter and in Chapter Eight. Moreover, some US BIDs— for example, one in Philadelphia—can issue their own debt;

- Investigate whether any of the purportedly large amounts of investment money available via pension and other funds could be channelled into UK projects. Generally the USA appears to be more innovative when it comes to raising money and is not so reliant on bank lending and equity. It was announced late in 2011 that the Coalition Government would launch a multibillion-pound investment programme aimed at getting the UK's economy moving. Most of this investment was to go into transportation projects. However, the majority of funding was to come from UK pension funds (BBC, 2011). Therefore it appears the UK is beginning to look for fresh methods of financing projects, but it could also consider international sources;

- Give greater autonomy to local authorities with regard to both raising money and decision-making about public procurement; and
- Make better use of PPPs in job creation, R&D and economic development/urban regeneration.

It was stated at the beginning of this book that academics in the USA are less critical of PPPs than their counterparts in the UK. Although this appears to have been contradicted by the literature review and some of the findings, it is argued that criticism in the USA is more directed at the flawed implementation or operation of a particular project. This differs from the criticism in the UK, which tends to be directed at the scheme itself. Geddes (2011) makes a valid point when he asks what PPPs are being compared with. Traditional procurement is sometimes referred to as if it were some kind of golden age of construction, when in reality there are huge problems with regard to cost and time overruns. It was highlighted by one of the interviewees (A4) that despite being responsible for only 15% of public procurement in the UK (HMT, 2006), PPPs are subject to much greater scrutiny than other arrangements. Perhaps if there is one thing the UK can learn from the USA it is to give PPPs a chance, or at least realise that some will fail without regarding the scheme itself as a failure. As one of the interviewees (PI3) stated, 'academics can come up with as many schemes as they like, but someone still has to pay for them'.

Appendix
Survey on the use of PPPs in the USA

1. Can you outline your background and previous experience in the context of Public-Private Partnerships (PPPs)?
2. What do you believe are the main objectives of PPPs?
3. What do you believe are the main drivers behind PPPs?
4. What are the key considerations when deciding whether to use a PPP or another method of service delivery?
5. How much autonomy does a state have when it comes to deciding whether to use a PPP?
6. Has the USA policy with respect to PPPs been influenced by that of other countries? If so, which countries have influenced it and how?
7. What lessons can be learnt from existing PPP projects in the USA?
8. How important do you believe the following factors are to the success of a PPP project?

   a. Project completed on time
   b. Value for money for the taxpayer
   c. Quality of design of PPP asset
   d. Aesthetic qualities of PPP asset
   e. Innovation
   f. Improved public-sector staff morale
   g. Improved public service delivery
   h. Quick tender process
   i. Smooth contract negotiations
   j. Good project management
   k. Good working relationships between all parties
   l. Profit   for the private-sector party
   m. Reduction of public-sector costs
   n. Fewer administrative duties for public-sector senior personnel
   o. Better resolution of maintenance problems
   p. Only way to get the asset built
   q. Transfer of risk to most appropriate party
   r. Other

9. How important do you believe the following potential drawbacks are in terms of limiting the overall success of a PPP project?

   a. Less flexibility in public-sector budgets (if portion ring-fenced to pay for service)
   b. Contract too rigid
   c. Poorer quality than expected
   d. Less innovation than expected
   e. Time-consuming process
   f. Limited information available
   g. Profits not shared between all parties
   h. Inexperience of public sector at contract negotiations
   i. Other

10. In your opinion what are the most important 'dos' and 'don'ts' of the PPP process?
11. PPPs appear to be more accepted in the USA than they are in the UK. Do you agree with this opinion and if so why?

References

Abdel Aziz, A. M. (2007), 'Successful Delivery of Public-Private Partnerships for Infrastructure Development', *Journal of Construction Engineering and Management*, Vol. 133, No. 12, pp. 918–931.

Accounting Standards Board (ASB) (1998), *Application Note F to Financial Reporting Standard 5, Reporting the Substance of Transactions*, London: ASB.

Ahlbrandt, R. S. Jr. (1990), 'The Revival of Pittsburgh—A Partnership between Business and Government', *Long Range Planning*, Vol. 23, No. 5, pp. 31–40.

Aldred, R. (2008), 'Managing Risk and Regulation within New Local 'Health Economies': The Case of NHS LIFT (Local Improvement Finance Trust)', *Health, Risk & Society*, Vol. 10, No. 1, pp. 23–36.

Allen, G. (2003), 'The Private Finance Initiative (PFI)', *Research Paper 03/79*, London: House of Commons Library, Economic Policy and Statistics Section.

American Bar Association (ABA) (2000), *The 2000 Model Procurement Code for State and Local Governments*, Chicago: ABA.

American Federation of Teachers (2001), *The Private Management of Public Schools: Analysis of the EAI Experience in Baltimore*, available at: www.aft.org/research/reports/private/eai1 (Accessed 11 April 2011).

Anon (2003), 'A Troubled Water Odyssey', *St. Petersburg Times*, 31 October, p. 14A.

Anon (2008), 'It's a Failure, but We Still Pay', *Star News Online*, available at: http://www.starnewsonline.com/article/20080110/EDITORIAL/801100347 (Accessed 17 November 2011).

Archeoembeault, W. G. and Deis, D. R. (1996), *Cost-Effective Comparisons of Private versus Public Prisons in Louisiana: A Comprehensive Analysis of Allen, Avoyelles and Winn Correctional Centers*, Baton Rouge: Louisiana State University.

Arthur Andersen (2000), *Value for Money Drivers in the Private Finance Initiative*, Report by Arthur Andersen and Enterprise LSE, Commissioned by the Treasury Taskforce.

Austin, J. and McCaffrey, A. (2002), 'Business Leadership Coalitions and Public-Private Partnerships in American Cities: A Business Perspective on Regime Theory', *Journal of Urban Affairs*, Vol. 24, No. 1, pp. 35–54.

Awofeso, N. (2007), 'Debate: Public-Private Health Partnerships in Prison Health Care—The Case for a Public Health Focus', *Public Money & Management*, Vol. 27, No. 5, pp. 305–306.

Balbach, E. D. and Glantz, S. A. (1998), 'Tobacco Control Advocates Must Demand High-Quality Media Campaigns: The California Experience', *Tobacco Control*, Vol. 7, No. 4, pp. 397–408.

Ball, R., Heafey, M. and King, D. (2000), 'Managing and Concluding the PFI Process for a New High School: Room for Improvement?', *Public Management*, Vol. 2, No. 2, pp. 159–180.

Ball, R., Heafey, M. and King, D. (2003a), 'Risk Transfer and Value for Money in PFI Projects', *Public Management Review*, Vol. 5. No. 2, pp. 279–290.

Ball, R., Heafey, M. and King, D. (2003b), 'Some Lessons from Using PFI for School Building Contracts', *Local Government Studies*, Vol. 29, No. 2, pp. 89–106.

Barker, C. (1996), *The Health Care Policy Process*, Thousand Oaks, CA: Sage.

Barnett, A. (1999), 'A Ruse by any Other Name', *Director*, Vol. 53, No. 3, p. 41.

Barringer, D. (2001), 'The New Urban Gamble', *The American Prospect*, 19 December, available at: http://prospect.org/article/new-urban-gamble (Accessed 20 April 2011).

Battaglio, R. P. and Khankarli, G. A. (2008), 'Toll Roads, Politics, and Public-Public Partnerships: The Case of Texas State Highway 121', *Public Works Management & Policy*, Vol. 13, No. 2, pp. 138–148.

Bayer, P. and Pozen, D. (2005), 'The Effectiveness of Juvenile Correctional Facilities: Public versus Private Management, *Journal of Law and Economics*, Vol. 48, No. 2, pp. 549–589.

Bazzoli, G. J., Stein, R., Alexander, J. A., Conrad, D. A., Sofaer, S. and Shortell, S. M. (1997), 'Public-Private Collaboration in Health and Human Service Delivery: Evidence from Community Partnerships', *The Milbank Quarterly*, Vol. 75, No. 4, pp. 533–561.

BBC (2010), *School Buildings Scheme Scrapped*, available at: http://www.bbc.co.uk/news/10514113 (Accessed 11 April 2011).

BBC (2011), *Multi-Billion Pound Push on UK Economy*, available at: http://www.bbc.co.uk/news/uk-15914145 (Accessed 16 December 2011).

Bloomfield, P. (2006), 'The Challenging Business of Long-Term Public-Private Partnerships: Reflections on Local Experience', *Public Administration Review*, Vol. 66, No. 3, pp. 400–411.

Bloomfield, P., Westerling, D. and Carey, R. (1998), 'Innovation and Risks in a Public–Private Partnership: Financing and Construction of a Capital Project in Massachusetts', *Public Productivity and Review*, Vol. 21, No. 4, pp. 460–471.

Blumer, H. (1969), *Symbolic Interactionism: Perspective and Method*, Englewood Cliffs, NJ: Prentice-Hall.

Boardman, A., Poschmann, F. and Vining, A. (2005), 'North American Infrastructure P3s: Examples and Lessons Learned', in Hodge, G. and Greve, C. (Eds.), *The Challenge of Public-Private Partnerships: Learning from International Experience*, Cheltenham: Edward Elgar.

Boyle, S. (1997), 'The Private Finance Initiative', *British Medical Journal*, Vol. 314, No. 7089, pp. 1214–1215.

Boyles, D. (2011), 'The Privatized Public: Antagonism for a Radical Democratic Politics in Schools?', *Educational Theory*, Vol. 61, No. 4, pp. 433–450.

Brinkerhoff, D. W. and Brinkerhoff, J. M. (2011), 'Public-Private Partnerships: Perspectives on Purposes, Publicness, and Good Governance', *Public Administration and Development*, Vol. 31, No. 1, pp. 2–14.

British BIDs (2011), *What Is a BID?*, available at: http://www.britishbids.info/AboutBIDs/WhatisaBID.aspx#AboutBIDs_BIDDev%20British%20Bids (Accessed 17 November 2011).

Broadbent, J., Gill, J. and Laughlin, R. (2008), 'Identifying and Controlling Risk: The Problem of Uncertainty in the Private Finance Initiative in the UK's National Health Service', *Critical Perspectives on Accounting*, Vol. 19, No. 1, pp. 40–78.

Brooks, H., Liebman, L. and Schelling, C. S. (Eds.) (1984), *Public-Private Partnership: New Opportunities for Meeting Social Needs*, Cambridge, MA: Bellinger.

Brooks, M. (2002), *Private Finance Initiative—Britain Leads the Way—To Disaster!*, available at: http://www.marxist.com/Economy/pfi.html (Accessed 11 April 2011).

Brown, K. (2007), 'Are Public-Private Transactions the Future of Infrastructure Finance?', *Public Works Management & Policy*, Vol. 12, No. 1, pp. 320–324.

Brown, T. L. and Potoski, M. (2003), 'Contract-Management Capacity in Municipal and County Governments', *Public Administration Review*, Vol. 63, No. 2, pp. 153–164.

Brown, T. L., Potoski, M. and Van Slyke, D. M. (2006), 'Managing Public Service Contracts: Aligning Values, Institutions, and Markets', *Public Administration Review*, Vol. 66, No. 3, pp. 323–331.

Burt, S. M. and Lessinger, L. M. (1970), *Volunteer Industry Involvement in Public Education*, Lexington, MA: D.C. Heath.

Byrne, P. F. (2005), 'Strategic Interaction and the Adoption of Tax Increment Financing', *Regional Science & Urban Economics*, Vol. 35, No. 3, pp. 279–303.

Cabral, S. (2007), 'On the Participation of Private Participation on Prisons Management: A New Institutional Economic Analysis', *O&S Organizações e Sociedade*, Vol. 14, No. 40, pp. 29–47.

Camp, S. and Daggett, D. (2005), 'Quality of Operations at Private and Public Prisons: Using Trends in Inmate Misconduct to Compare Prisons', *Justice Research and Policy*, Vol. 7, No. 1, pp. 27–51.

Castro, G. and Stillman, C. (2005), 'Clean Air', in Castro, G. and Stillman, C. (Eds.), *Chavez: A Taxing Burden* (pp. 1–3), available at: http://www.cleanhouston.org/air/features/chavez.htm (Accessed 7 October 2011).

Centers for Disease Control and Prevention (1999), *Best Practices for Comprehensive Tobacco Control Programs—August 1999*, Atlanta, GA: US Department of Health and Human Services, Centers for Disease Control and Prevention, National Center for Chronic Disease Prevention and Health Promotion, Office on Smoking and Health.

Chapin, T. (2002), 'Beyond the Entrepreneurial City: Municipal Capitalism in San Diego', *Journal of Urban Affairs*, Vol. 24, No. 5, pp. 565–581.

Clarke, T. (2003), 'Priming the Pump: The Emerging Debate over Water Privatization in North America', *PA Times*, Vol. 26, No. 1, p. 9.

Clavel, P. and Kraushaar, R. (1998), 'On Being Unreasonable: Progressive Planning in Sheffield and Chicago', *International Planning Studies*, Vol. 3, No. 2, pp. 143–162.

Commission for Architecture and the Built Environment (CABE) (2002), *Client Guide: Achieving Well Designed Schools through PFI*, London: CABE.

Commission on Public Private Partnerships (2001), *Building Better Partnerships*, London: Institute of Public Policy Research.

Commonwealth of Massachusetts, Office of the Inspector General (2001), *Privatization of Wastewater Facilities in Lynn, Massachusetts*, available at: http://www.mass.gov/ig/publ/lynnwwrp.pdf (Accessed 29 April 2011).

Connolly, C., Martin, G. and Wall, A. P. (2008), 'Education, Education, Education: The Third Way and PFI', *Public Administration*, Vol. 86, No. 4, pp. 951–968.

Connolly, C. and Wall, A. P. (2009), *Public Private Partnerships in Ireland: Benefits, Problems and Critical Success Factors*, Dublin: The Institute of Chartered Accountants in Ireland.

Connolly, C. and Wall, A. P. (2011), 'The Global Financial Crisis and UK PPPs', *International Journal of Public Sector Management*, Vol. 24, No. 6, pp. 533–542.

Crowley, W. F. Jr., Sherwood, L., Salber, P., Scheinberg, D. Slavkin, H., Tilson, H., Reece, E. A., Catanese, V., Johnson, S. B., Dobs, A., Genel, M., Korn, A., Reame, N., Bonow, R., Grebb, J. and Rimoin, D. (2004), 'Clinical Research in the United

States at a Crossroads: Proposal for a Novel Public-Private Partnership to Establish a National Clinical Research Enterprise', *Journal of the American Medical Association*, Vol. 291, No. 9, pp. 1120–1126.

Daniel, D. E. (2008), 'Lessons Learned from Public-Private Partnerships for Infrastructure', *Public Works Management & Policy*, Vol. 13, No. 2, pp. 89–91.

Deller, S. C., Hinds, D. G. and Hinman, D. L. (2001), 'Local Public Services in Wisconsin: Alternatives for Municipalities with a Focus on Privatization', *Department of Agricultural and Applied Economics Staff Paper No. 441*, University of Wisconsin-Madison, available at: http://www.aae.wisc.edu/pubs/sps/pdf/stpap441.pdf (Accessed 20 April 2011).

Desilets, B. (2009), *Florida I-595. PPP Financing during the Crisis*, available at: http://www.cdfa.net/cdfa/cdfaweb.nsf/fbaad5956b2928b086256efa005c5f78/6 e82c94dee1   521b2862575fb00689748/$FILE/Claret%20PPP%20Article%20 June%202009.pdf (Accessed 5 October 2011).

Detrick, S. (1999), 'The Post Industrial Revitalization of Pittsburgh: Myths and Evidence', *Community Development Journal*, Vol. 34, No. 1, pp. 4–12.

DiNapoli, T. P. (2011), *Controlling Risk without Gimmicks: New York's Infrastructure Crisis and Public-Private Partnerships*, available at: http://www.osc.state.ny.us/reports/infrastructure/pppjan61202.pdf (Accessed 5 December 2011).

Dumort, A. (2000), 'New Media and Distance Education: An EU–US Perspective', *Information, Communication & Society*, Vol. 3, No. 4, pp. 546–556.

Dunn, J. A. Jr., (1999), 'Transportation: Policy-Level Partnerships and Project-Based Partnerships', *American Behavioral Scientist*, Vol. 43, No. 1, pp. 92–106.

Edwards, P. and Shaoul, J. (2002), 'Controlling the PFI Process in Schools: A Case Study of the Pimlico Project', *Policy & Politics*, Vol. 31, No. 3, pp. 371–385.

Edwards, P. and Shaoul, J. (2003), 'Partnerships: For Better for Worse?', *Accounting, Auditing and Accountability Journal*, Vol. 16, No. 3, pp. 397–421.

Edwards, P., Shaoul, J., Stafford, A. and Arblaster, L. (2004), *Evaluating the Operation of PFI in Roads and Hospitals*, London: Association of Chartered Certified Accountants.

Egnew, R. C. and Baler, S. G. (1998), 'Developing Principles, Goals, and Models for Public/Private Partnerships', *Administration and Policy in Mental Health*, Vol. 25, No. 6, pp. 571–580.

Engel, E., Fischer, R. and Galetovic, A. (2001), 'Least Present Value of Revenue Auctions and Highway Franchising', *The Journal of Political Economy*, Vol. 109, Vol. 5, pp. 993–1020.

Engel, E., Fischer, R. and Galetovic, A. (2006), 'Privatizing Highways in the United States', *Review of Industrial Organization*, Vol. 29, Nos. 1/2, pp. 27–53.

Engel, E., Fischer, R. and Galetovic, A. (2011), 'Public-Private Partnerships to Revamp U.S. Infrastructure', *The Hamilton Project Discussion Paper*, Washington, DC: The Brookings Institute.

Erie, S. P., Kogan, V. and MacKenzie, S. A. (2010), 'Redevelopment, San Diego Style: The Limits of Public-Private Partnerships', *Urban Affairs Review*, Vol. 45, No. 5, pp. 644–678.

Ewoh, A. I. E. (2007), 'Public-Private Partnerships in a Texas Municipality: The Case of the City of Houston Tax Increment Reinvestment Zones', *Public Works Management & Policy*, Vol. 12, No. 1, pp. 359–369.

Ewoh, A. I. E., and Dillard, T. (2003), 'Public-Private Partnerships in Houston and Seattle Urban Municipalities', *Journal of Public Management & Social Policy*, Vol. 9, No. 1, pp. 31–41.

Federal Highway Administration (FHwA), (2004), *2004 Status of the Nation's Highways, Bridges, and Transit: Conditions and Performance (Report to Congress)*, Washington, DC: U.S. Department of Transportation.

FHwA (2005a), *Synthesis of Public-Private Partnership Projects for Roads, Bridges and Tunnels from around the World 1985–2004*, Washington, DC: U.S. Department of Transportation.

FHwA (2005b), *Partnerships in Transportation Workshops (Final Report)*, Washington, DC: U.S. Department of Transportation.

FHwA (2006), *Current Toll Road Activity in the U.S.*, available at: http://www.fhwa.dot.gov/ppp/index.htm (Accessed 22 April 2011).

FHwA (2007), *PPPs Model Legislation*, available at: http://fhwainter.fhwa.dot.gov/ppp/legislation.htm (Accessed 22 April 2011).

Financial Reporting Advisory Board (FRAB) (2007), *Accounting for PPP Arrangements Including PFI Contracts*, London: FRAB.

Fitz, J. and Beers, B. (2002), 'Education Management Organisations and the Privatisation of Public Education: A Cross-National Comparison of the USA and Britain', *Comparative Education*, Vol. 38, No. 2, pp. 137–154.

Forrer, J. and Kee, J. E. (2003), 'Public Servants as Contract Managers', *Public Contract Law Journal*, Vol. 33, No. 2, pp. 361–367.

Forrer, J., Kee, J. E., Newcomer, K. E. and Boyer, E. (2010), 'Public-Private Partnerships and the Public Accountability Question', *Public Administration Review*, Vol. 70, No. 3, pp. 475–484.

Frieden, B. J., and Sagalyn, L. B. (1989), *Downtown Inc.: How America Rebuilds Cities*, Cambridge, MA: MIT Press.

Froud, J. (2003), 'The Private Finance Initiative: Risk, Uncertainty and the State', *Accounting, Organizations and Society*, Vol. 28, No. 6, pp. 567–589.

Furtwengler, C. B. (1998a), 'Heads Up! The EMOs Are Coming', *Educational Leadership*, Vol. 56, No. 2, pp. 44–47.

Furtwengler, C. B. (1998b), 'Policies and Privatisation', *The American School Board Journal*, Vol. 185, No. 4, pp. 42–46.

Gaffney, D. and Pollock, A. (1999), 'Pump Priming the PFI: Why Are Privately Financed Hospital Schemes Being Subsidised?', *Public Money & Management*, Vol. 17, No. 3, pp. 11–16.

Gaffney, D., Pollock, A. M., Price, D. and Shaoul, J. (1999), 'PFI in the NHS: Is There an Economic Case?', *British Medical Journal*, Vol. 319, No. 7202, pp. 116–119.

Gallay, D. R. (2006), 'Public-Private Partnerships for Financing Federal Capital: Useful or Chimerical?', *Public Works Management Policy*, Vol. 11, No. 2, pp. 139–151.

Gapper, J. (2008), 'On the Pot-Holed Highway to Hell', *Financial Times*, 7 May.

Garvin, M. J. (2010), 'Enabling Development of the Transportation Public-Private Partnership Market in the United States', *Journal of Construction Engineering and Management*, Vol. 136, No. 4, pp. 402–411.

Geddes, R. R. (2011), *The Road to Renewal: Private Investment in U.S. Transportation Infrastructure*, Washington, DC: American Enterprise Institute for Public Policy Research.

Ghere, R. (2001a), 'Probing the Strategic Intricacies of Public-Private Partnership: The Patent as a Comparative Reference', *Public Administration Review*, Vol. 61, No. 4, pp. 441–451.

Ghere, R. (2001b), 'Ethical Futures and Public-Private Partnerships: Peering Far Down the Track', *Public Organization Review*, Vol. 1, No. 3, pp. 303–319.

Girard, P., Mohr, R. D., Deller, S. C. and Halstead, J. M. (2009), 'Public-Private Partnerships and Cooperative Agreements in Municipal Service Delivery', *International Journal of Public Administration*, Vol. 32, No. 5, pp. 370–392.

Greuling, J. E. (1987), 'Tax Increment Financing: A Downtown Development Tool', *Economic Development Review*, Vol. 5, No. 1, pp. 23–27.

Grimsey, D. and Lewis, M. K. (2004), *Public Private Partnerships: The Worldwide Revolution in Infrastructure Provision and Project Finance*, Cheltenham: Edward Elgar.

Grimsey, D. and Lewis, M. K. (2005), 'Are Public Private Partnerships Value for Money? Evaluating Alternative Approaches and Comparing Academic and Practitioner Views', *Accounting Forum*, Vol. 29, No. 4, pp. 345–378.

Guppy, P. (2003), *Private Prisons and the Public Interest: Improving Quality and Reducing Cost through Competition*, Washington, DC: Washington Policy Center.

Halai, I. (2009), 'Landmark Floridian Deal Reaches Financial Close', *Infrastructure Journal Online*, 4 March, available at: http://www.ijonline.com (Accessed 5 October 2011).

Halsey III, A. (2011), 'Va. Officials Reach Tentative Deal for I-95 HOT Lanes', *The Washington Post*, 6 December, available at: http://www.washingtonpost.com/local/va-officials-reach-tentative-deal-for-i-95-hot-lanes/2011/12/06/gIQAbq14aO_story.html (Accessed 16 December 2011).

Hart, O. (2003), 'Incomplete Contracts and Public Ownership: Remarks and an Application to Public-Private Partnerships', *The Economic Journal*, Vol. 113, No. 486, pp. 69–76.

Hart, O., Shleifer, A. and Vishny, R. W. (1997), 'The Proper Scope of Government: Theory and an Application to Prisons, *Quarterly Journal of Economics*, Vol. 112, No. 4, pp. 1127–1161.

Hatcher, R. (2006), 'Privatization and Sponsorship: The Re-agenting of the School System in England', *Journal of Education Policy*, Vol. 21, No. 5, pp. 599–619.

Hazelroth, S. C. (2010), *Testimony before the House Ways and Means Committee Subcommittee on Select Revenue Measures*, available at: http://waysandmeans.house.gov/media/pdf/111/2010May13_Hazelroth_Testimony.pdf (Accessed 5 October 2011).

Heald, D. (2003), 'Value for Money Tests and Accounting Treatment in PFI Schemes', *Accounting, Auditing and Accountability Journal*, Vol. 16, No. 3, pp. 342–371.

Heald, D. and Geaughan, N. (1997), 'Accounting for the Private Finance Initiative', *Public Money & Management,* Vol. 17, No. 3, pp. 11–16.

Heald, D. and Georgiou, G. (2011), 'The Substance of Accounting for Public-Private Partnerships', *Financial Accountability & Management*, Vol. 27, No. 2, pp. 217–247.

Hedgpeth, D. (2011a), 'Airports Board Wants State, Feds to Contribute More Money for Dulles Rail', *The Washington Post*, 17 August, available at: http://www.washingtonpost.com/local/airports-board-wants-state-feds-to-contribute-more-money-for-dulles-rail/2011/08/17/gIQAYGVCMJ_story.html (Accessed 16 December 2011).

Hedgpeth, D. (2011b), 'Parties Reach Financing Deal on Phase 2 of Dulles Rail', *The Washington Post*, 10 November, available at: http://www.washingtonpost.com/local/parties-reach-financing-deal-on-dulles-rail/2011/11/10/gIQA2mFIAN_story.html (Accessed 16 December 2011).

Hellowell, M. and Pollock, A. M. (2009), 'Non-Profit Distribution: The Scottish Approach to Private Finance in Public Services', *Social Policy and Society*, Vol. 8, No. 3, pp. 405–418.

Henderson, J. and McGloin, E. (2004), 'North/South Infrastructure Development via Cross-Border PPP Mechanisms', *The International Journal of Public Sector Management*, Vol. 17, No. 5, pp. 389–413.

Her Majesty's Treasury (HMT) (1999), *PFI Technical Note No. 1 (Revised): How to Account for PFI Transactions*, London: HMT.

HMT (2003), *PFI: Meeting the Investment Challenge*, Norwich: The Stationery Office.

HMT (2006), *PFI: Strengthening Long Term Partnerships*, Norwich: The Stationery Office.

Hibbert, L. (2000), 'A Private Function', *Professional Engineering*, Vol. 131, No. 14, pp. 40–41.

Hill, R. P. (2002), 'Service Provision through Public-Private Partnerships: An Ethnography of Service Delivery to Homeless Teenagers', *Journal of Service Research*, Vol. 4, No. 4, pp. 278–289.

Hirtt, N. (2000), 'The Millennium Round and the Liberalisation of the Education Market', *Education & Social Justice*, Vol. 2, No. 2, pp. 220–235.

Hobbs, H. (2011), 'Fairfax County High Schools: Private Funding Necessary to Turf Fields', *The Washington Post*, 16 November, available at: http://www.washingtonpost.com/local/fairfax-county-high-schools-private-funding-neccessary-to-turf-fields/2011/11/14/gIQAtgqBRN_story.html (Accessed 16 November 2011).

Hodge, G. A. (2004), 'The Risky Business of Public-Private Partnerships', *Australian Journal of Public Administration*, Vol. 63. No. 4, pp. 37–49.

Hodge, G. A. and Greve, C. (2007), 'Public-Private Partnerships: An International Performance Review', *Public Administration Review*, Vol. 67, No. 3, pp. 545–558.

Hodges, R. and Mellett, H. (1999), 'Accounting for the Private Finance Initiative in the United Kingdom National Health Service', *Financial Accountability & Management*, Vol. 15, Nos. 3/4, pp. 275–290.

Hodges, R. and Mellett, H. (2004), 'Reporting PFI in Annual Accounts: A User's Perspective', *Public Money & Management*, Vol. 24, No. 3, pp. 153–158.

Holeywell, R. (2011), 'The Indiana Toll Road: A Model for Privatization?', *Governing*, October, available at: http://www.governing.com/topics/mgmt/indiana-toll-road-model-privatization.html (Accessed 5 October 2011).

Honadle, B. W. (1983), *Public Administration in Rural Areas and Small Jurisdictions: A Guide to the Literature*, New York: Garland Publishing Company.

Honadle, B. W. (2001), 'Theoretical and Practical Issues of Local Government Capacity in an Era of Devolution', *Journal of Regional Analysis and Policy*, Vol. 31, No. 1, pp. 77–90.

Hood, J., Asenova, D., Bailey, S. and Manochin, M. (2007), 'The UK's Prudential Borrowing Framework: A Retrograde Step in Managing Risk?', *Journal of Risk Research*, Vol. 10, No. 1, pp. 49–66.

Hood, J., Fraser, I. and McGarvey, N. (2006), 'Transparency of Risk and Reward in UK Public-Private Partnerships', *Public Budgeting & Finance*, Vol. 26, No. 4, pp. 40–58.

House of Lords (2010), 'Private Finance Projects and Off-Balance Sheet Debt', *Select Committee on Economic Affairs, 1st Report of Session 2009–10*, London: The Stationery Office.

Houston, T. (2002), 'Public–Private Partnerships: A Successful Model in Tobacco Control', *Addiction*, Vol. 97, No. 8, pp. 959–960.

Houston Independent School District (HISD) (1995), *Community Partnerships Catalog*, Houston, TX: HISD.

Hui, G. and Hayllar, M. R. (2010), 'Creating Public Value in E-government: A Public-Private-Citizen Collaboration Framework in Web 2.0', *The Australian Journal of Public Administration*, Vol. 69, No. S1, pp. S120–S131.

Hurst, C. and Reeves, E. (2004), 'An Economic Analysis of Ireland's First Public Private Partnership', *The International Journal of Public Sector Management*, Vol. 17, No. 5, pp. 379–388.

Iida, E. E., Springer, J. F., Pecora, P. J., Bandstra, E. S., Edwards, M. C. and Basen, M. M. (2005), 'The SESS Multisite Collaborative Research Initiative: Establishing Common Ground', *Child and Family Social Work*, Vol. 10, No. 3, pp. 217–228.

International Financial Reporting Interpretations Committee (IFRIC) (2007), *IFRIC 12, Service Concession Arrangements*, IFRIC.

International Financial Services London (IFSL) (2009), *PFI in the UK & PPP in Europe 2009*, London: IFSL.

Istrate, E. and Puentes, R. (2011), *Moving Forward on Public Private Partnerships: U.S. and International Experience with PPP Units*, Washington, DC: The Brookings Institute.

Jaffe, A. B. (1998), 'The Importance of "Spillovers" in the Policy Mission of the Advanced Technology Program', *Journal of Technology Transfer*, Vol. 23, No. 2, pp. 11–19.

Johnson, R. A. and Walzer, N. (1996), *Competition for City Services: Has the Time Arrived? Privatization in Illinois Municipalities*, Macomb, IL: Illinois Institute for Rural Affairs, available at: http://www.iira.org/pubsnew/publications/IIRA_RRR_87.pdf (Accessed 11 April 2011).

Kamieniecki, S., Shafie, D. and Silvers, J. (1999), 'Forming Partnerships in Environmental Policy: The Business of Emissions Trading in Clean Air Management', *The American Behavioral Scientist*, Vol. 43, No. 1, pp. 107–123.

Kasarda, J. D. and Rondinelli, D. A. (1998), 'Innovative Infrastructure for Agile Manufacturers', *Sloan Management Review*, Vol. 39, No. 2, pp. 73–82.

Ke, Y., Wang, S., Chan, A. P. C. and Cheung, E. (2009), 'Research Trend of Public-Private Partnership in Construction Journals', *Journal of Construction Engineering and Management*, Vol. 135, No. 10, pp. 1076–1086.

Kee, J. E. and Forrer, J. (2008), 'Private Finance Initiative—The Theory behind the Practice', *International Journal of Public Administration*, Vol. 31, No. 2, pp. 151–167.

Kee, J. E. and Newcomer, K. E. (2008), *Transforming Public and Nonprofit Organizations: Stewardship for Leading Change*, McLean, VA: Management Concepts.

Kennedy, S. S. and Rosentraub, M. S. (2000), 'Public-Private Partnerships, Professional Sports Teams, and the Protection of the Public's Interests', *American Review of Public Administration*, Vol. 30, No. 4, pp. 436–459.

Kettl, D. F. (1987), *Third-Party Government and the Public Manager: The Changing Forms of Government Action*, Washington, DC: National Academy of Public Administration.

Kirk, R. J. and Wall, A. P. (2001), 'Substance, Form and PFI Contracts', *Public Money & Management*, Vol. 21, No. 3, pp. 41–46.

Kirk, R. J. and Wall, A. P. (2002), 'The Private Finance Initiative: Has the Accounting Standards Board Reduced the Scheme's Value for Money?', *Public Management Review*, Vol. 4 No. 4, pp. 529–547.

Krol, R. and Svorny, S. (2004), 'The Collapse of a Noble Idea', *Regulation*, Vol. 27, No. 4, pp. 30–33.

Kunreuther, H. (2000), 'Insurance as Cornerstone for Public-Private Sector Partnerships', *Natural Hazards Review*, Vol. 1, No. 2, pp. 126–136.

Kunreuther, H. and Roth, R. Sr. (Eds.) (1998), *Paying the Price: The Status and Role of Insurance against Natural Disasters in the United States*, Washington, DC: Joseph Henry Press.

Laffont, J. J. and Tirole, J. (1988), 'Repeated Auctions of Incentive Contracts, Investment and Bidding Parity, with an Application to Takeovers', *Rand Journal of Economics*, Vol. 19, No. 4, pp. 515–537.

Lanza-Kaduce, L., Parker, K. and Thomas, C. (1999), 'A Comparative Recidivism Analysis of Releases from Private and Public Prisons', *Crime and Delinquency*, Vol. 45, No. 1, pp. 28–47.

Lari, A., Levinson, D., Zhao, Z., Iacono, M., Aultman, S., Vardhan Das, K. Junge, J., Larson, K. and Scharenbroich, M. (2009), *Value Capture for Transportation Finance: Technical Research Report*, Minneapolis, MN: Centre for Transportation Studies, University of Minnesota.

Lawther, W. C. (2004), 'Public Outreach for Public-Private Partnerships: The Case of Advanced Traveler Information Systems', *Public Works Management Policy*, Vol. 9, No. 2, pp. 120–131.

Lawther, W. C. (2005), 'Public-Private Partnerships in Transportation Policy: The Case of Advanced Traveler Information Systems', *International Journal of Public Administration*, Vol. 28, No. 13, pp. 1117–1134.

Lazard (2010), *Public Private Partnerships: Presentation to NABE*, available at: http://www.nabe.com/rt/reg/documents/Lazard.pdf (Accessed 14 November 2011).

Leinberger, C. B. and Doherty, P. C. (2010), 'The Next Real Estate Boom', *Washington Monthly*, November, available at: http://www.brookings.edu/articles/2010/11_real_estate_leinberger.aspx (Accessed 21 November 2011).

Levin, H. M. (1999), 'The Public-Private Nexus in Education', *The American Behavioral Scientist*, Vol. 43, No. 1, pp. 124–137.

Levine, M. V. (2000), 'A Third-World City in the First World: Social Exclusion, Racial Inequality and Sustainable Development in Baltimore, Maryland', in Polese, M. and Stren, R. (Eds.) *The Social Sustainability of Cities: Diversity and the Management of Change*, Toronto: University of Toronto Press.

Levinson, D. M. and Istrate, E. (2011), *Access for Value: Financing Transportation through Land Value Capture*, Washington, DC: The Brookings Institute.

Levy, S. M. (1996), *Build, Operate, Transfer*, New York: Wiley.

Levy, S. M. (2008), 'Public-Private Partnerships in Infrastructure', *Leadership and Management in Engineering*, Vol. 8, No. 4, pp. 217–230.

Link, A. (1999), 'Public/Private Partnerships in the United States', *Industry and Innovation*, Vol. 6, No. 2, pp. 191–217.

Link, A. N., Paton, D. and Siegel, D. S. (2002), 'An Analysis of Policy Initiatives to Promote Strategic Research Partnerships', *Research Policy*, Vol. 31, Nos. 8/9, pp. 1459–1466.

Link, A. N. and Scott, J. T. (2001), 'Public/Private Partnerships: Stimulating Competition in a Dynamic Market', *International Journal of Industrial Organization*, Vol. 19, No. 5, pp. 763–794.

Lockwood, S. C. (1995), 'Public-Private Partnerships in US Highway Finance: ISTEA and Beyond', *Transportation Quarterly*, Vol. 49, No. 1, pp. 5–26.

Longoria, T. Jr. (1999), 'The Distribution of Public-Private Partnerships: Targeting of Voluntary Efforts to Improve Urban Education', *Nonprofit and Voluntary Sector Quarterly*, Vol. 28, No. 3, pp. 315–329.

Lonsdale, C. and Watson, G. (2007), 'Managing Contracts under the UK's Private Finance Initiative: Evidence from the National Health Service', *Policy & Politics*, Vol. 35, No. 4, pp. 683–700.

Los Angeles Community Development Bank (LACDB) (1999), *Annual Business Plan*, Los Angeles, CA: LACDB.

Love, A. A. (1998), 'Study: Nursing Homes Screen Workers Poorly', *Houston Chronicle*, 6 September, p. 3A.

Lovrich, N. P. Jr. (1999), 'Policy Partnering between the Public and Not-for-Profit Private Sectors: A Key Policy Lever or a Dire Warning of Difficulty Ahead?', *The American Behavioral Scientist*, Vol. 43, No. 1, pp. 177–191.

Lukemeyer, A. and McCorkle, A. (2006), 'Privatization of Prisons: Impact on Prison Conditions', *American Review of Public Administration*, Vol. 36, No. 2, pp. 189–206.

Maltby, P. (2003), *Comparing Cost*, available at: http://www.publicservice.co.uk/pdf/pfi/summer2003/PJ41%20Paul%20Maltby%20ATL.pdf (Accessed 10 September 2007).

Man, J. Y. and Rosentraub, M. S. (1998), 'Tax Increment Financing: Municipal Value Growth', *Public Finance Review*, Vol. 26, No. 6, pp. 523–547.

Mansell, W. (2001), 'Parents Oppose Privatisation', *Times Educational Supplement*, 9 March, p. 9.

Maryland Department of Transportation (2011), *Baltimore-Washington Rail Intermodal Facility*, available at: http://www.mdot.maryland.gov/Planning/ICTF/Home.html (Accessed 21 November 2011).

Maskin, E. and Tirole, J. (2008), 'Public-Private Partnerships and Government Spending Limits', *International Journal of Industrial Organization*, Vol. 26, No. 2, pp. 412–420.

Mayston, D. (1999), 'The Private Finance Initiative in the National Health Service: An Unhealthy Development in New Public Management?', *Financial Accountability and Management*, Vol. 15, Nos. 3/4, pp. 249–274.

McCabe, W., McKendrick, J. and Keenan, J. (2001), 'PFI in Schools—Pass or Fail?', *Journal of Finance and Management in Public Services*, Vol. 1, No. 1, pp. 63–74.

McFadyean, M. and Rowland, D. (2002), *PFI vs. Democracy: School Governors and the Haringey Schools PFI Scheme*, London: Menard Press.

McQuaid, R. W. and Scherrer, W. (2010), 'Changing Reasons for Public-Private Partnerships (PPPs)', *Public Money & Management*, Vol. 30, No. 1, pp. 27–34.

McWilliam, J. (1997), 'A Commissioner's Tale: Avery Hill Student Village, University of Greenwich', *Public Money & Management*, Vol. 17, No. 3, pp. 21–24.

Minow, M. (2003), 'Public and Private Partnerships: Accounting for the New Religion', *Harvard Law Review*, Vol. 116, No. 5, pp. 1229–1270.

Mitchell, M. (2003), *The Pros of Privately-Housed Cons: New Evidence on the Cost Savings of Private Prisons*, Tijeras, NM: Rio Grande Foundation.

Molnar, A. (1996), *Giving Kids the Business: The Commercialization of America's Schools*, Boulder, CO: Westview Press.

Montague, E. (2003), *Prison Health Care: Healing a Sick System through Private Competition*, Seattle: Washington Policy Centre.

Morallos, D, Amekudzi, A., Ross, C. and Meyer, M. (2009), 'Value for Money Analysis in U.S. Transportation Public-Private Partnerships', *Transportation Research Record: Journal of the Transportation Research Board*, No. 2115, pp. 27–36.

Morland, L., Duncan, J., Hoebing, J., Kirschke, J. and Schmidt, L. (2005), 'Bridging Refugee Youth and Children's Services: A Case Study of Cross-Service Training', *Child Welfare*, Vol. 84, No. 5, pp. 791–812.

Morris, C. (2007), 'Government and Market Pathologies of Privatization: The Case of Prison Privatization', *Politics & Policy*, Vol. 35, No. 2, pp. 318–341.

Moulton, L. and Anheier, H. K. (2001), 'Public-Private Partnerships in the United States: Historical Patterns and Current Trends', *Civil Society Working Paper 16*, London: The Centre for Civil Society, Department of Social Policy, London School of Economics and Political Science.

Mullen, L. (1998), 'NFL's Next New Team May Pay Lower Entry Fee', *Street and Smith's Sports Business Journal*, Vol. 1, No. 20, p. 7.

National Audit Office (NAO) (1997), 'The Skye Bridge', *HC5, Parliamentary Session 1997–1998*, London: The Stationery Office.

NAO (1999), 'The United Kingdom Passport Agency: The Passport Delays of Summer 1999', *HC 812, Parliamentary Session 1998–1999*, London: The Stationery Office.

NAO (2003a), 'PFI: Construction Performance', *HC 371, Parliamentary Session 2002–2003*, London: The Stationery Office.

NAO (2003b), 'The Operational Performance of PFI Prisons: Report by the Comptroller and Auditor General', *HC 700, Parliamentary Session 2002–2003*, London: The Stationery Office.

National Conference of State Legislators (NCSL) (2011), *Public-Private Partnerships for Transportation: A Toolkit for Legislators (Updated Version)*, Denver, CO/Washington, DC: NCSL.

National Council for Public-Private Partnerships (NCPPP) (2002), 'For the Good of the People: Using Public-Private Partnerships to Meet America's Essential Needs', *A White Paper on Partnerships by NCPPP*, Washington, DC: NCPPP.

NCPPP (2004), *Lackland Air Force Base Privatized Housing Project, Frank Tejeda Estates*, available at: http://www.ncppp.org/cases/lackland.html (Accessed 11 April 2011).

NCPPP (2005), *Creating Effective Public-Private Partnerships for Buildings and Infrastructure in Today's Economic Environment*, available at: http://ncppp.org/resources/papers/HDRP3whitepaper.pdf (Accessed 11 April 2011).

NCPPP (2011a), *New York Avenue Metro Station, Washington DC*, available at: http://www.ncppp.org/cases/nystation.shtml (Accessed 16 November 2011).

NCPPP (2011b), *Union Station Metro Station, Washington DC*, available at: http://www.ncppp.org/cases/unionstation.shtml (Accessed 16 November 2011).

Newcombe, T. (2011), 'Quincy, Mass., Rebuilds from Scratch', *Governing*, October, available at: http://www.governing.com/columns/urban-notebook/quincy-mass-rebuilds-from-scratch.html (Accessed 5 December 2011).

Nisar, T. M. (2007), 'Risk Management in Public-Private Partnership Contracts', *Public Organization Review*, Vol. 7, No. 1, pp. 1–19.

North Carolina GlobalTransPark (2011), *Global TransPark Tenants*, available at: http://www.ncgtp.com/tenants.html (Accessed 11 April 2011).

Northern Ireland Audit Office (2004), *Building for the Future: A Review of the PFI Education Pathfinder Projects*, London: The Stationery Office.

Oakley, D. (2006), 'The American Welfare State Decoded: Uncovering the Neglected History of Public-Private Partnerships. A Case Study of Homeless and Relief Services in New York City: 1920s and 1990s', *City & Community*, Vol. 5, No. 3, pp. 243–267.

Office of Technology Policy (1996), *Effective Partnering: A Report to Congress on Federal Technology Partnerships*, Washington, DC: US Department of Commerce.

Organisation for Economic Co-operation and Development (OECD) (2008), *Public-Private Partnerships: In Pursuit of Risk Sharing and Value for Money*, Paris: OECD.

Ortiz, I. N. and Buxbaum, J. N. (2008), 'Protecting the Public Interest in Long-Term Concession Agreements for Transportation Infrastructure', *Public Works Management & Policy*, Vol. 13, No. 2, pp. 126–137.

Osborne, S. (2001), *Public-Private Partnerships: Theory and Practice in International Perspective*, New York: Routledge.

Page, S. N., Ankner, W., Jones, C. and Fetterman, R. (2008), 'The Risks and Rewards of Private Equity in Infrastructure', *Public Works Management & Policy*, Vol. 13, No. 2, pp. 100–113.

Palast, G. (2000), 'Profit and Education Don't Mix', *Observer Business Section*, 26 March, p. 7.

Pantelias, A. and Zhang, Z. (2010), 'Methodological Framework for Evaluation of Financial Viability of Public-Private Partnerships: Investment Risk Approach', *Journal of Infrastructure Systems*, Vol. 16, No. 4, pp. 241–250.

Papajohn, D., Cui, Q. and Bayraktar, M. E. (2011), 'Public-Private Partnerships in U.S. Transportation: Research Overview and a Path Forward', *Journal of Management in Engineering*, Vol. 27, No. 3, pp. 126–135.

Patterson, J. A. (2004), 'What's the Bottom Line? Corporate Involvement in an Early Childhood Initiative', *Urban Review*, Vol. 36, No. 2, pp. 147–168.

Patton, M. Q. (1990), *Qualitative Evaluative Research Methods*, Thousand Oaks, CA: SAGE.

Peters, B. G. (1998), ' "With a Little Help from Our Friends": Public-Private Partnerships as Institutions and Instruments', in Pierre, J. (Ed) *Partnerships in Urban Governance*, New York: St Martin's Press.

Peters, B. G. and Pierre, J. (1998), 'Governance without Government? Rethinking Public Administration', *Journal of Public Administration Research and Theory*, Vol. 8, No. 2, pp. 223–243.

Pollitt, M. G. (2000), 'The Declining Role of the State in Infrastructure Investments in the UK', University of Cambridge, Department of Applied Economics, Working Paper 0001.

Pollock, A. M., Dunnigan, M., Gaffney, D., Price, D. and Shaoul, J. (1999), 'Planning the "New" NHS: Downsizing for the 21st Century', *British Medical Journal*, Vol. 319, No. 7203, pp. 179–184.

Pollock, A. M. and Price, D. (2008), 'Has the NAO Audited Risk Transfer in Operational Private Finance Initiative Schemes?', *Public Money & Management*, Vol. 28, No. 3, pp. 173–178.

Pollock, A., Price, D., and Dunnigan, M. (2000), *Deficits before Patients: A Report on the Worcestershire Royal Infirmary PFI and Worcestershire Hospital Configuration*, London: School of Public Policy, University College London.

Pollock, A. M., Shaoul, J. and Vickers, N. (2002), 'Private Finance and "Value for Money" in NHS Hospitals: A Policy in Search of a Rationale?', *British Medical Journal*, Vol. 324, No. 7347, pp. 1205–1209.

Poole, R. W. Jr. (2006), 'A Response to Critics of Toll Road Leasing', *Public Works Financing*, Vol. 205, May, p. 3.

Preston, D. (2010), *Morgan Stanley Group's $11 Billion Makes Chicago Taxpayers Cry*, Bloomberg, available at: http://www.bloomberg.com/news/2010–08–09/morgan-stanley-group-s-11-billion-from-chicago-meters-makes-taxpayers-cry.html (Accessed 5 October 2011).

Price, B. and Riccucci, N. (2005), 'Exploring the Determinants of Decisions to Privatize State Prisons', *American Review of Public Administration*, Vol. 35, No. 3. pp. 223–235.

Public Works Financing (PWF) (2010), *2010 International Survey of Public Private Partnerships*, Westfield, NJ: PWF.

Rand Corporation (1999), *Use of Public-Private Partnerships to Meet Future Army Needs*, Santa Monica, CA: Rand Corporation.

Reason Foundation (2006), *Transforming Government through Privatization—Reflection from Pioneers in Government Reform (Annual Privatization Report)*, Los Angeles: Reason Foundation.

Renckens, S. (2008), 'Yes, We Will! Voluntarism in US E-Waste Governance', *Review of European Community and International Environmental Law*, Vol. 17, No. 3, pp. 286–299.

Renzi, M. and Kelly, B. (1991), 'Plymouth County as Entrepreneur', *Plymouth County Business Review*, Vol. 10, No. 2, p. 3.

Ricaurte, J. L., Arboleda, C. A. and Peña-Mora, F. (2008), 'Civil Engineers in Public-Private Partnerships and as Master Planners for Infrastructure Development', *Leadership and Management in Engineering*, Vol. 8, No. 4, pp. 276–286.

Rikowski, G. (2003), 'Schools and the GATS Enigma', *Journal for Critical Education Policy Studies*, Vol. 1, No. 1, available at: http://www.jceps.com/index.php?pageID=article&articleID=8 (Accessed 11 April 2011).

Rom, M. C. (1999), 'From Welfare State to Opportunity, Inc.: Public-Private Partnerships in Welfare Reform', *American Behavioral Scientist*, Vol. 43, No. 1, pp. 155–176.

Romzek, B. and Johnston, J. M. (2002), 'Effective Contract Implementation and Management: A Preliminary Model', *Journal of Public Administration Research and Theory*, Vol. 12, No. 3, pp. 423–453.

Rosenau, P. V. (1999), 'Introduction: The Strengths and Weaknesses of Public-Private Policy Partnerships', *The American Behavioral Scientist*, Vol. 43, No. 1, pp. 10–34.

Rosenbaum (1999), 'The Good Lessons of Bad Experience: Rethinking the Future of Commercial Nuclear Power', *The American Behavioral Scientist*, Vol. 43, No. 1, pp. 74–91.

Rosentraub, M. (1997), *Major League Losers: The Real Costs of Sports and Who's Paying for It*, New York: Basic Books.

Rosentraub, M. (1998), 'Why Baseball Needs New York to Just Say No', *The Nation*, Vol. 267, No. 5, pp. 20–26.

Rubin, J. (2011), 'Perry's Job Model', *The Washington Post*, 18 August, available at: http://www.washingtonpost.com/blogs/right-turn/post/perrys-job-model/2011/03/29/gIQATVjcNJ_blog.html (Accessed 5 October 2011).

Rubin, J. S. and Stankiewicz, G. M. (2001), 'The Los Angeles Community Development Bank: The Possible Pitfalls of Public-Private Partnerships', *Journal of Urban Affairs*, Vol. 23, No. 2, pp. 133–153.

Sagalyn, L. B. (2007), 'Public/Private Development', *Journal of the American Planning Association*, Vol. 75, No. 1, pp. 7–22.

Salamon, L. M. (1981), 'Rethinking Public Management: Third Party Government and the Changing Forms of Government Action', *Public Policy*, Vol. 29, pp. 255–275.

Saltman, R. B. and Figueras, J. (1998), 'Analyzing the Evidence on European Health Care Reform', *Health Affairs*, Vol. 17, No. 2, pp. 85–108.

Schneider, A. L. (1999), 'Public Private Partnerships in the U.S. Prison System', *The American Behavioral Scientist*, Vol. 43, No. 1, pp. 192–208.

Schuman, R. and Sherer, E. (2001), *In ATIS U.S. Business Models Review*, Washington, DC: U.S. Department of Transportation and ITS Joint Program Office.

Schuster, C. and Lundstrom, W. (2002), 'Public-Private Partnerships in International Trade: A Lobbying Effort from Passive to Aggressive in the USA?', *Journal of Public Affairs*, Vol. 2, No. 3, pp. 125–135.

Schweitzer, H., Alderman, M. L. and Bayh, E. (2011), 'We Already Have the Infrastructure Bank We Need', *The Washington Post*, 29 September, available at: http://www.washingtonpost.com/opinions/we-already-have-the-infrastructure-bank-we-need/2011/09/27/gIQA59TI8K_story.html (Accessed 5 October 2011).

Scottish Futures Trust (2011), *Welcome*, available at: http://www.scottishfuturestrust.org.uk/ (Accessed 29 September 2011).

Scribner, M. (2011), *The Limitations of Public-Private Partnerships: Recent Lessons from the Surface Transportation and Real Estate Sectors*, Washington, DC: Competitive Enterprise Institute.

Seely, B. E. (1987), *Building the American Highway System: Engineers as Policy Makers*, Philadelphia: Temple University Press.

Shaoul, J., Stafford, J. and Stapleton, P. (2008), 'The Cost of Using Private Finance to Build, Finance and Operate Hospitals', *Public Money & Management*, Vol. 28, No. 2, pp. 101–108.

Shields, D. C. (2011), 'A Public-Private Partnership: American Water's Revolutionary Water Reuse System for the Patriots' Home', *Global Business and Organizational Excellence*, Vol. 30, No. 5, pp. 56–63.

Siemiatycki, M. (2010), 'Delivering Transportation Infrastructure through Public-Private Partnerships: Planning Concerns', *Journal of the American Planning Association*, Vol. 76, No. 1, pp. 43–58.

Silk, H., Gusha, J., Adler, B., Sachs Leicher, E., Finison, L. J., Huppert, M. E., Stille, S. and Yost, J. B. (2010), 'The Central Massachusetts Oral Health Initiative (CMOHI): A Successful Public–Private Community Health Collaboration', *Journal of Public Health Dentistry*, Vol. 70, No. 4, pp. 308–312.

Sofge, E. (2009), 'Why Shovel-Ready Infrastructure Is Wrong (Right Now)', *Popular*

Mechanics, 5 February, available at: http://www.popularmechanics.com/technology/engineering/infrastructure/4302578 (Accessed 21 November 2011).

Sparer, M. S. (1999), 'Myths and Misunderstandings: Health Policy, the Devolution Revolution, and the Push for Privatization', *The American Behavioral Scientist*, Vol. 43, No. 1, pp. 138–154.

Spielman, D. J. and von Grebmer, K. (2006), 'Public-Private Partnerships in International Agricultural Research: An Analysis of Constraints', *Journal of Technology Transfer*, Vol. 31, No. 2, pp. 291–300.

Stainback, J. (2000), *Public/Private Finance and Development: Methodology Deal Structuring Developer Solicitation*, New York: Wiley.

Stavins, R. N. (1998), 'What Can We Learn from the Grand Policy Experiment? Lessons from SO2 Allowance Trading', *Journal of Economic Perspectives*, Vol. 12, No. 3, pp. 69–88.

Stewart, J. (2000), *The Nature of British Local Government*, Basingstoke: Macmillan.

Stiglitz, J. E. and Wallsten, S. J. (1999), 'Public-Private Technology Partnerships: Promises and Pitfalls', *The American Behavioral Scientist*, Vol. 43, No. 1, pp. 52–73.

Supiot, A. (1996), 'Work and the Public/Private Dichotomy', *International Labour Review*, Vol. 135, No. 6, pp. 3–22.

Taylor, T. C., Kistler, W. P. and Citron, B. (2008), 'Economic Public Private Partnerships for Development', *American Institute of Physics Conference Proceedings*, Vol. 969, pp. 533–540.

Texas Comptroller of Public Accounts (2004), *Biennial Reports of Reinvestment Zone for Tax Abatement Registry, Tax Abatement Agreement, and Tax Increment Financing Zone Registry*, Austin, TX: Texas Comptroller of Public Accounts.

Timmins, N. (1999), 'Rescue Plan for Royal Armouries', *Financial Times*, 2 August.

Toll Road News (2010), *South Bay Expressway Company Files for Bankruptcy in San Diego*, available at: http://www.tollroadsnews.com/node/4664 (Accessed 5 October 2011).

United Nations General Assembly (2005), *Enhanced Cooperation between the United Nations and All Relevant Partners, in Particular the Private Sector*, Report of the Secretary-General, A/60/214.

US Department of Justice (2009), 'Prisoners in 2008', *Bureau of Justice Statistics Bulletin, Office of Justice Programs*, December.

US Department of Transportation (USDOT), ITS Joint Program Office (2000), *511 for Traveler Information Implementation Issues*, Washington, DC: USDOT.

US General Accounting Office (GAO) (1997), *Social Service Privatization: Expansion Poses Challenges in Ensuring Accountability for Program Results (GAO/HEHS-98-6)*, Washington, DC: GAO.

US GAO (2003), *Budget Issues: Alternative Approaches to Finance Federal Capital (GAO-03-1011)*, Washington, DC: GAO.

Vining, A. R. and Boardman, A. E. (2008), 'Public-Private Partnerships: Eight Rules for Governments', *Public Works Management & Policy*, Vol. 13, No. 2, pp. 149–161.

Vining, A. R., Boardman, A. E. and Poschmann, F. (2005), 'Public-Private Partnerships in the US and Canada: "There Are No Free Lunches"', *Journal of Comparative Policy Analysis*, Vol. 7, No. 3, pp. 199–220.

von Zielbauer, P. (2007), 'As Health Care in Jails Go Private, 10 Days Can Be a Death Sentence', *The New York Times*, 27 February.

Wall, A. P. and Martin, G. (2003), 'Best Value: How Local Authorities in Northern Ireland Are Consulting with Stakeholders', *Journal of Finance & Management in Public Services*, Vol. 3, No. 2, pp. 15–30.

Walton, C. M., and Euritt, M. A. (1990), 'Highway Finance and the Private Sector: Issues and Alternatives', *Transportation Research*, Vol. 24A, No. 4, pp. 265–276.

West, A. and Currie, P. (2008), 'The Role of the Private Sector in Publicly Funded Schooling in England: Finance, Delivery and Decision Making', *Policy & Politics*, Vol. 36, No. 2, pp. 191–207.

Wettenhall, R. (2003), 'The Rhetoric and Reality of Public-Private Partnerships', *Public Organization Review*, Vol. 3, No. 1, pp. 77–107.

Whitfield, D. (2005), 'Building Schools for Shareholders', *Red Pepper*, available at: http://www.redpepper.org.uk/KYE/x-kye-Jan2005.html (Accessed 10 September 2007).

Whitfield, D. (2006), 'The Marketisation of Teaching', *The PFI Journal*, Vol. 52, March, pp. 92–93.

Whitty, G., Edwards, T. and Gewirtz, S. (1993), *Specialisation and Choice in Urban Education: The City Technology Colleges Experiment*, London: Routledge.

Wilkey, P. L. (2000), 'Public/Private Partnerships to Renew the Industrial Landscape', *Public Works Management & Policy*, Vol. 4, No. 3, pp. 248–255.

World Trade Organisation (2002), *Council for the Trade in Services—Education Services–Background Note by the Secretariat*, available at: http://docsonline.wto.org/gen (Accessed 11 April 2011).

Yancey, G., Rogers, R., Singletary, J., Atkinson, K. and Thomas, M. L. (2004), 'Public-Private Partnerships: Interactions between Faith-Based Organizations and Government Entities', *The Social Policy Journal*, Vol. 3, No. 4, pp. 5–17.

Zhang, X. (2004), 'Concessionaire Selection: Methods and Criteria', *Journal of Construction Engineering and Management*, Vol. 130, No. 2, pp. 235–244.

Zimbalist, A. (1998), 'A Scary Thought: Jones May Be Right about Browns', *Street and Smith's Sports Business Journal*, Vol. 1, No. 20, p. 7.

Index